REVELATION
to
Transformation

How Seeing Jesus Will Change Your Life

PAUL WHITE

WestBow
PRESS
A DIVISION OF THOMAS NELSON

WestBow Press books may be ordered through booksellers or by contacting:

WestBow Press
A Division of Thomas Nelson
1663 Liberty Drive
Bloomington, IN 47403
www.westbowpress.com
1-(866) 928-1240

ISBN: 978-1-4497-1901-2 (sc)
ISBN: 978-1-4497-1902-9 (hc)
ISBN: 978-1-4497-1900-5 (e)

Library of Congress Control Number: 2011930634

Printed in the United States of America

WestBow Press rev. date: 06/01/2011

Acknowledgements

I would like to extend special thanks to my friends Russell and Andrea Cross for their early review of the first few chapters and their encouragement to go on. Also, thanks goes to Amanda Casey for her editing and organization of the overall manuscript. Where the book flows and makes sense, it is to her credit. Where it does not, I take all the blame.

To Midland Church, you are a pastor's dream.

To my parents, Rick and Lovetia White, who have showed me what ministry is all about and have always been my biggest supporters.

To my brother Michael: you and me buddy, all the way.

To the love of my life, my wife, NaTasha. It would take a book much larger than this one for me to convey all you mean to me. You are the most obvious proof that I am highly favored.

Contents

"Sir, We Would See Jesus" | *1*

Charles H. Spurgeon, a preacher from the nineteenth century, said that it was his goal in preaching to take a text and follow it like a road until it led him to Christ and His cross. If the text from which he was preaching did not seem to lead in that direction, he would simply jump over to another Scripture that did.

I may share few qualities with the late, great Spurgeon, but I do share his desire to have my sermons lead to Jesus. In a time when mankind is looking all around to find help and hope, I believe that the answer *Remember* has already been given. Together, I want us to go on a journey toward a place where we are free from the vice and failures that have defined us. Not content to put on a different appearance or to change other people's perceptions of us, but to actually *be* different than we have ever been.

We will deal with religion and relationship in full detail in the next chapter, but let me begin our journey by acknowledging why many of you have made the decision to read this book. I concede some are reading to learn what I might think of Scripture or to become familiar with my ministry, but I pray many more of you were drawn to the book out of a desire to change something about your life. It is to you that I focus my attention throughout these pages. I understand the longing to change, and I can tell you early on, *change is possible.*

Now, if you are looking to change your physical appearance or your mental capacity, move on to a different book. I have no diet tips, exercise advice, or investment information. I don't even have practical steps for changing the way you act. In no way is this book about teaching you to change your performance, so let it be said very clearly: *this book is not about behavior modification.* The change I speak of is a change of heart.

I realize that many of you are believers in Christ and have had a born-again experience. For those of us who call ourselves Christians, it is difficult to conclude that we need to change anything but our behavior. We know our hearts were changed when we accepted Christ, and it is for this reason we have become accustomed to hearing sermons and teaching that focus on what *we* need to do in order to change. This has led to focusing on modifying our behavior to line up with the change that Christ made in us at conversion.

"But don't you think changing our behavior is important?"

I *do* think changing our behavior is important, since our behavior serves as a window to the world of who our Jesus is. However, please note that I have no intention of teaching you how to modify your behavior, as I believe man *cannot* modify it permanently. I don't want to attack your behavior, but rather inform you of the things leading to the behavior. If we adjust those areas, I believe that your behavior will follow suit.

"Sir, we would see Jesus!"

> "And there were certain Greeks among them that came up to worship at the feast: the same came therefore to Philip, which was of Bethsaida of Galilee, and desired him, saying, 'Sir, we would see Jesus'" (John 12:20, 21 King James Version).

This verse is my personal mandate every time I step into the pulpit. I see these Greek men, strangers to the Jewish faith, hungry to meet the man they have heard so much about. They chose to speak to Philip, perhaps because of his Greek-sounding name, in order to have someone present their case to the Master. They wanted nothing more than to, "see Jesus," and it reminds me that men are still seeking as much today.

The pulpits in our churches are full of all kinds of preaching. It varies as much in content as it does in style. I know, because I've used different styles and different content! By my own account, it seems much of it is man-centered, concentrated on teaching the listener how to fix his life. While the methods are different from church to church, the means are very similar: sin is pointed to and, exposed, and the offender is reprimanded. We are then told to do better through various programs. All in all, we are put the through the wringer of guilt and condemnation, shamed into either getting it right or getting left behind! This constant preaching and teaching of guilt and condemnation are pulling people's eyes off of the loveliness of Jesus and His finished work and onto the unfinished areas of their lives. [X]

We know that we are flawed; we don't need someone screaming at us to figure that out. Our problem is not the absence of the knowledge that we need help; rather, it is the utter inability to help ourselves. Calvary was God's intervention in all of our issues. By relieving us of the punishment of sin, He is freeing us from the weight of guilt and from the fear of death. The author of Hebrews said that when Jesus died He did so to, "release those who through fear of death were all their lifetime subject to bondage" (Hebrews 2:15). Jesus has delivered us from fear of eternal punishment by being punished in our place!

Regarding the men seeking Jesus in John 12, we may not be like these Greeks in our heritage or nationality, but we are very much like them in another way. While "Greek" tells us where they are from, in biblical terminology it tells us much more, as Jewish writers referred to all non-Jews as either Greeks or barbarians (see Romans 1:14, 16). At the close of this chapter, we will see what the end result was for both the seekers and for us.

For whatever reason you are reading, let my intentions be crystal clear. I intend to unveil to you the loveliness of my Jesus so you see Him as I believe the Word presents Him. He is perfectly beautiful, and only He holds the power to change your life. As we see Him together, we are seeing our destiny held firmly in His hands, and all modification of behavior is sure to come as a result of an encounter with Jesus. *Good!*

The Dividing Line of Scripture

Did you know the dividing line of the Bible is not the blank page between the Old Testament and the New Testament? That page divides the two Testaments, but it does not give us a clear change in the way God dealt with man. The division point of Scripture was an important point in the ministry of the apostle Paul, as he mentioned in his letter to the young pastor Timothy.

> "Be diligent to present yourself approved to God, a worker who does not need to be ashamed, rightly dividing the word of truth" (2 Timothy 2:15).

Obviously, if there is a right way to divide the Word, there must be a wrong way. Our job is to differentiate between what falls on one side of the

3

Word and what falls on the other. In doing so, we are pulling out truths within the context of each Testament to find how they apply in our lives.

Context

This is a good time to mention a very important point that will surface time and time again throughout the course of this book. When we read a particular Scripture, it is vital that we remember the context of it. In other words, we damage the integrity of a text when we take a verse and act as if it stands alone. The verses in front of and behind the text affect its meaning, and acting as if they are not there will often lead to the twisting of Scriptures.

Be careful not to make Scripture fit into your doctrine; rather, make sure your doctrine fits into Scripture. As you and I journey toward transformation together, an abundance of Scripture to support or destroy our case is absolutely essential. This is why we will constantly resort back to the text to find out what it is actually saying to us.

Another thing that determines context is a proper knowledge as to whom and about what the Scripture was written. Sometimes we can find this information in the first few verses of a book (like the book of James, for instance), or we can simply look at the title (e.g., Hebrews). Other times, a more intensive study is necessary, and though it may be time consuming, it is of supreme importance if we are going to fulfill Paul's mandate to, "rightly divide the Word."

Treasures in the New and the Old

In speaking to the Jews in the book of Matthew, Jesus concluded a long section of parables dealing with the Kingdom. He asked the listeners if they understood everything, to which they answered in the affirmative. He then brought out this beautiful truth:

> "Therefore every scribe instructed concerning the kingdom of heaven is like a householder who brings out of his treasure things new and old" (Matthew 13:52).

Scribes were experts of Jewish law, which is found in what we call the Old Testament. Jesus states that with His arrival, every scribe should be bringing out of the treasure chest of the Old Testament things both new and old. Notice He doesn't say, "old and new," which makes sense, considering "old" should come before "new." Instead, He emphasizes the "new," over the "old," giving higher praise to the new revelations found in Him and His work. These new revelations are found by scribes, meaning that there are powerful revelations of Jesus found within the confines of the Old Testament. How wonderful to begin to see Jesus in the same places where one had only seen the law!

Christ Himself made a further division of Scripture in His parable of garments and bottles. He stated, "No one puts a piece from a new garment on an old one; otherwise the new makes a tear, and also the piece that was taken out of the new does not match the old. And no one puts new wine into old wineskins; or else the new wine will burst the wineskins and will be spilled, and the wineskins will be ruined. But new wine must be put into new wineskins, and both are preserved" (Luke 5:36–38). He certainly means more than clothing and drink! This is another illustration of the difference in the Old and the New Testaments. Just as there are revelations of both new and old, there is also a separation in the two as well.

Now, back to the topic at hand: what is the dividing line of Scripture? If all of the Old Testament was a treasure chest of information regarding Jesus (which we will see plenty more of as we proceed in later chapters), it would make logical sense that the dividing line would be the arrival of Jesus. This is why we break up the Bible at His arrival and insert that blank page between the books of Malachi and Matthew. However, Jesus gives us the answer, starkly drawing the line in the biblical sand, at His *death*, not at His birth.

"So when Jesus had received the sour wine, He said, 'It is finished!' And bowing His head, He gave up His spirit" (John 19:30).

What is "it" in the phrase, "It is finished?" It is more than His life and His crucifixion. The "it" to which Jesus refers is all of the Old Testament and the way God dealt with mankind through the covenant He had cut with Moses at Mt. Sinai. In short, the great war against sin, which had been fought since the Garden of Eden, was finally over. Now, everything after the dividing line of, "It is finished," can be seen through the lens of what we refer to as "the finished work." Paul knew it, believed it, and preached it:

"For I determined not to know anything among you except Jesus Christ and Him crucified" (1 Corinthians 2:2).

Opening Questions

As I have already done once in this chapter, I will occasionally insert a question that I think some of you may wish to have answered. Some of these questions will argue the opposing viewpoint or show ways that we have taken some Scriptures and twisted them out of context. I use this method of writing so I can make my point in a more personal way, as many of these questions were once my own or have been posed to me by people over the years.

Both Testaments open in a similar manner, posing questions that set the tone for the reader who is inquisitive enough to ask them. Discounting a facetious question posed by the snake to Eve in the Garden, let's look at the first question in the Old Testament and the first question in the New Testament. The results speak volumes about rightly dividing the Word of God.

1. Old—"Then the LORD God called to Adam and said to him, *'Where are you?'*" (Genesis 3:9).

2. New—"Now after Jesus was born in Bethlehem of Judea in the days of Herod the king, behold, wise men from the East came to Jerusalem, saying, *'Where is He* who has been born King of the Jews?'" (Matthew 2:1, 2).

These questions address the heartbeat of each Testament. The first is God calling to Adam, showing the downfall of man and his struggle to come back to God. The second is man calling to God, looking for the promised Messiah. In the journey to answer both questions, we encounter Jesus, the answer for all wayward souls and the end result of our search.

Let's learn to filter everything we read in the Scriptures through what Christ did to finish the work at the cross. This allows us to place everything on one side or the other of the biblical dividing line. Where Jesus finished the work marks the end of the Old Covenant and the beginning of the New Covenant. Though we don't abandon the Old Testament, may we no longer use it as a book of lists and instructions, but we read it to find the treasure that is Jesus, our Pearl of Great Price!

A simple study tool I have learned to use in preparing a sermon is to ask a certain question about every story or Scripture that I encounter. That question is: what did the cross do to change this? If Jesus truly finished the work, and the Old Testament is leading us up to that moment, reading

Scripture without the cross on the horizon is to discern improperly what the text is trying to convey. Together, you and I are going to keep the finished work of Christ on the cross in our crosshairs, so to speak, so that we don't miss the beauty of our Jesus.

"Pastor Paul, I'm having no problem with seeing Jesus or discerning His finished work; I am just simply under a curse. My difficulty is a long-standing problem passed down to me from previous generations. I need deliverance!"

If that statement epitomizes how you feel, I would concur that you need deliverance but not from a curse! You need deliverance from the kind of thinking that says Jesus didn't pay it all at the cross and that you are still beneath the forces of darkness.

My friend, if you have received Christ as your Savior, you have a brand new Father, and believe me, He passed no such curse to you.

"Christ has redeemed us from the curse of the law, having become a curse for us (for it is written, 'Cursed is everyone who hangs on a tree')" (Galatians 3:13).

Make yourself familiar with that verse, for you will see it again. It gives us a solid promise that Jesus has bought us out from under the curse, due to the fact that He was made to be a curse for us. Our problem is not what our father or mother did that has been passed on to us. We are not who we are because our grandparents made us that way. We not only have a brand-new Father; He has changed our hearts to have a complete spiritual renovation.

"Not by works of righteousness which we have done, but according to His mercy He saved us, through the washing of regeneration and renewing of the Holy Spirit" (Titus 3:5).

Catch the power of that phrase, "the washing of regeneration," because it is of key importance. We have been washed in the blood of Jesus, and in essence, we became "re-gened." Our spiritual DNA is not what it used to be, because *we are not who we used to be.*

"Doesn't the Old Testament say that the sins of the fathers are visited upon the children? Doesn't this guarantee that their sins pass on to all of us?"

The Bible does indeed say that, and it is found in God's list of Ten Commandments He gave to Moses on Mt. Sinai. In the Second Commandment, He declares that man shall not make any carved image to bow down to. Then He makes this promise:

> "I, the LORD your God, am a jealous God, visiting the iniquity of the fathers upon the children to the third and fourth generations of those who hate Me" (Exodus 20:5).

This provides us with a perfect opportunity to ask our question, "What did the cross do to change this?" The Scripture sounds pretty cut and dry: whatever the fathers did wrong, God pours wrath upon the children. However, the verse I recommended you to get familiar with a moment ago comes into play right here. Christ became the curse for us (Galatians 3:13); therefore, whatever curse was destined to come our way has landed on Him.

> "Like a flitting sparrow, like a flying swallow, so a curse without cause shall not alight" (Proverbs 26:2).

Jesus has become the curse for all of us, so any curse that is destined for us is now considered, "without cause," thus the Word promises that it "shall not alight." Though Exodus 20 gives us cause to believe we should be judged for our father's sins, Galatians 3 assures us that the cross has made a difference. This is not a case of the Bible working against itself, but rather, it is a prime example of the finished work making a difference!

The framework has been laid for our journey together, one of having Christ revealed to us in all of His loveliness so that we can be transformed into His image. We are ready to read Scriptures within their context and to rightly divide the Word, quick to find out what the cross of Christ has done to change our situation. Prepare your heart to see the power of God's great exchange, and prepare your life to never be the same!

The Power of the Exchanged Life | 2

Do you remember being asked in your childhood what you want to be when you grow up? It seems like a common icebreaker when dealing with young people, because the answer to the question gives insight into how people think and what their influences are. Some will answer doctor, others baseball player or movie star. But I have never heard anyone answer, "I want to be religious when I grow up," though most of us end up that way in one form or the other.

Let me say first and foremost that I know what it means to be religious. I understand the feeling of inadequacy and the constant nagging in your head that you haven't done enough to be pleasing to God. I know what it means to read the Bible out of obligation, thinking that it is what a "good Christian" should do. I am well aware of the sense of guilt and condemnation that overwhelms a person when he falls short of some sort of religious standard. I have put money in the offering plate, because I was convinced that I would be cursed by God if I did not. I have prayed an hour a day, because I "knew" that there would be no wisdom or anointing in my life if I could not "tarry one hour." I have gone to church when I was too sick to move, because I was scared to, "forsake the assembly." If anyone knows the self-inflicted weight and burden of religion, I do.

This burden eventually became so heavy that I didn't think I could survive. The harder I tried, the harder it became; and the more that I did to be right, the more I actually did wrong. Overwhelmed by the load of performance-based Christianity, I came to a crossroads: either God had to show me a way to live free, or I had to give up altogether. What I didn't realize was that the answer was not one way or the other but a combination of both.

I began to realize something that now seems so obvious, and I hope to make it seem that way to you. Every religion in the world is basically structured the same way: you do your best by following a list of rules and regulations, and in the end, you hope to be right with God. You can slap whatever label you want on it, but most of it comes down to one question: how hard are you working?

This is when God began to reveal to me the unique place that Christianity holds among the other religions of the world. True Christianity, where Christ suffered and died in our place, completely and totally excludes the works of man. "Relationship" becomes the key word, replacing "religion," causing us to focus not on our efforts but on establishing a growing relationship with a loving God.

The relationship is best displayed in Christianity's most extraordinary and unique quality: the sovereign God became a man so that He could pay for man's inabilities and sins through His own sacrificial death. Other religions require the sacrifice, effort, and even death of their adherents, while Christianity has the deity performing all of the effort and laying down His own life for the followers.

Armed with that knowledge, my faith steadily grew to include the good news that if God made me and then became a man to save me, it must be God's priority to do all the work. Simply put, I began to believe that God made me, so God had to change me! Freed from the obligation of changing myself, I was able to sit back and let God do the changing only He could do.

Part of our religious heritage is built on our desire to *do* something. If we have a problem in our physical or domestic lives, we know there are certain things that must be done to fix that problem. Difficulty comes when we bring that attitude into our spirit man, assuming that there are things we can do or stop doing that will change who we are or how we feel. This is natural, seeing as we are spiritually pre-programmed to be busy.

When Adam ate of the forbidden fruit, he died spiritually and then passed that death on to all of us. Thus, our very nature is to sin, "as by one man sin entered into the world, and death by sin" (Romans 5:12). But do you recall the name of the tree from which Adam ate? It was the Tree of Knowledge of Good and Evil, meaning that when he ate from it, he would have the knowledge of the difference between good and evil. That doesn't sound so bad, right? What could possibly be wrong with knowing the difference between what is right and what is wrong? If we know this, surely we can do the right thing and avoid the wrong. In this lies the trap!

The knowledge of what is right and wrong provided Adam with no help to do the right and avoid the wrong, trapping him in a system of works by which he would always try to live. Our first father introduced us to religion, effectively binding us to a life lived by our conscience, where we try day and night to get back to the place that he had so easily lost. Even his day-to-day bread would now be acquired by the sweat of his own labor, making all of his spiritual blessings come by the same means (Genesis 3:19).

Before we go any further, I want to remind you of one often missed fact from the Garden experience. Sin was not born out of a rebellious spirit on Adam and Eve's part, for they had no rebellion in their hearts. Satan's trick in getting Eve to eat the fruit (which led to Adam eating it as well) was to lead her to believe that God had withheld some of His righteousness and knowledge from her. He said to Eve, "For God knows that in the day you eat of it your eyes will be opened, and you will be like God, knowing good and evil" (Genesis 3:5). Eve ate because she wanted to be more righteous, not to be rebellious. Religion never intends to do wrong but is always designed to make us better. Unfortunately, as Eve quickly learned, there is no righteousness to be found in works.

Now that we are born with the nature to sin inside of us, we have certain tendencies and habits that prevail over us, whether we like it or not. One man finds it impossible to resist alcohol, while another can't control his temper. One woman struggles with envy and jealousy in her heart, while another is under the addiction to drugs and is powerless to be free. These people often place their hope in religious activity, but after a while, they find that, not only are they still in bondage, but they are also wracked by guilt and regret.

The Apostle Paul experienced this type of failure; he wrote that the more he tried to do right, the more he did wrong (Romans 7:15). He grew so incensed at his own mistakes that he cried out in desperation, "Who will deliver me from this body of death?" (Romans 7:24). He was smart enough to know that these actions would lead to death, and his deliverance was going to come through a person. His conclusion was, "I thank God through Jesus Christ our Lord" (verse 25). Paul had learned that religion and works were leaving him frustrated, and victory would only come through someone else doing the work for him.

When we see a loved one who has a problem, we call an intervention and try to confront the person so that he will be motivated to take steps toward improvement. God saw that mankind had myriad problems, so

He did an intervention of His own. He became flesh and dwelled among men. He lived all of the rules and ordinances of the law perfectly and then took the punishment that was destined for fallen man into Himself and died so that men could go free. This action culminated at the cross, where Jesus suffered shame and humiliation before crying out, "It is finished." We refer to this as the finished work, because Jesus finished the work of our redemption there. We introduced the term, "the finished work," in the opening chapter, but it will surface often throughout this book, as our transformation from who we were into who we want to be starts and stops at His finished work.

The act of the finished work on the cross was God paying for the debt caused by sin. He was literally paying for us to have His glory working through us, as we had lost that with Adam's fall. Paul wrote that "all have sinned and fall short of the glory of God" (Romans 3:23), while the Jerusalem Bible says that when we sinned we, "forfeited God's glory." What we forfeited in sin, Christ got back through His finished work!

Since you and I actually fell from glory through our representative Adam, it became possible for us to be recovered by a second representative, which was Jesus. Paul said it this way:

> "Therefore, as through one man's offense judgment came to all men, resulting in condemnation, even so through one Man's righteous act the free gift came to all men, resulting in justification of life. For as by one man's disobedience many were made sinners, so also by one Man's obedience many will be made righteous" (Romans 5:18, 19).

By declaring the world guilty (condemned) through one man's fall (Adam's), God could justly declare the world righteous through one man's (Jesus') obedience. Due to this important rule, Christianity is not about "not sinning," but it is about letting Christ live His perfect life through us. It is, "the obedience of one," that makes you and me righteous. Praise God!

Please let this sink in, as it is a pivotal statement about our understanding of Christ's finished work: *Jesus did not come only to change men's lives but rather to exchange His perfect righteousness for all of our imperfections.* There is no Christian "self-help" program in which we change ourselves, for our problems are too deep-rooted in our first father, Adam. Since we can't change, we need a new life with a new start. This is the provision of the Great Exchange, where we are made alive by His life.

"For if when we were enemies we were reconciled to God through the death of His Son, much more, having been reconciled, we shall be saved by His life" (Romans 5:10).

Look at the last phrase in the previous verse: "we shall be saved by His life." Are we saved by our lives? Are we saved from hell by our good deeds or our hard work? Are we made better by our reading, praying, giving, or attending? No! We are actually saved and changed from who we were into His righteousness by His life flowing through us.

Now, let's take a look at a key verse in the New Testament that gives us the foundation of this wonderful exchange that God made with us:

"For He made him who knew no sin to be sin for us, that we might become the righteousness of God in Him" (2 Corinthians 5:21).

This is one of my favorite verses in the entire Bible. It says so much to me about how loved and favored that I must be, and I want it to become just as personal to you. This shows us that God made Jesus to be sin, even though Jesus never committed any sins of His own. By making Jesus to be sin, He can't see that sin in me anymore, giving me the very righteousness of God due to my faith in the finished work. Do you see the Great Exchange? Jesus was made to be sin so that you could be made the righteousness of God in Christ. Hallelujah!

"Pastor Paul, this Scripture doesn't mean that Jesus actually became sin, just that He carried our sin."

Honestly, I used to share that point of view. I believed that because Jesus never committed sin, it was somehow sacrilegious for me to believe that God actually viewed my sin *in* Jesus at the cross. I would have told you that Jesus *carried* my sins so that I could *carry* His righteousness. With this interpretation, one must also believe that Christ's righteousness is something you can put on and take off, like you put on a coat. This idea led me to believe that if I committed a sin, my righteousness vanished, while if I did things that were pleasing to God, I was again clothed in righteousness. This is why I preached and believed that in order to be seen as righteous in God's eyes, you had to be doing certain things and avoiding others. I viewed Christianity as the carrying of God's righteousness through actions and works. How is this any different than Islam or Buddhism or even Judaism?

Admittedly, we can't build the doctrine of God's Great Exchange program through the finished work on only one verse, so let's add another:

> "For what the law could not do it in that it was weak through the flesh, God did by sending His own Son in the likeness of sinful flesh, on account of sin: He condemned sin in the flesh (Romans 8:3).

Paul is showing us that our flesh is too weak to keep the demands of the law, so God sent Jesus in a flesh that was very much like ours. He was not exactly like us, because His Father was not of this earth, as the Virgin birth ensured that Jesus would be born without the nature to sin. Being free from any sin of His own, He thus becomes qualified to have our sins placed in His flesh. Notice that our sin is not "carried" by Jesus but rather placed, "in the flesh." This allowed God to condemn our sin in the body of Jesus.

In the next chapter, we explore in detail how God dealt with our sins in the body of His Son. For now, I hope you receive the glorious revelation that with your sins condemned in the body of Jesus, there remains no more condemnation for you (Romans 8:1). God can't condemn sin twice, or He would not be just. See your sins as having been condemned in Jesus and then rest assured that God won't condemn them in you! If your sins are in Jesus and you have believed in Him by faith, His righteousness must be in you.

How about one more verse regarding the exchange?

> "Who Himself bore our sins in His own body on the tree, that we, having died to sins, might live for righteousness by whose stripes you were healed" (1 Peter 2:24).

Again we see that our sins were actually *in* the body of Christ, "on the tree," meaning that Jesus had our sins put into Him on the cross. Now that we have placed our faith in Christ, we are dead to the old nature of sin, which allows us to let His righteousness come out of us daily. Since there has been a death, there can now be a resurrection, meaning that since we have identified with Christ by faith in His finished work, He can now live His life through us. Paul said it this way:

> "Therefore we were buried with Him through baptism into death, that just as Christ was raised from death by the glory of the Father, even so we also should walk in newness of life ... Now if we

died with Christ, we believe that we shall also live with Him ... Likewise you also, reckon yourselves to be dead indeed to sin, but alive to God in Christ Jesus our Lord" (Romans 6:4, 8, 11).

Sometimes we lose the power and authority of some Scriptures by placing them in situations they do not belong. For instance, the previous verses are often used to support water baptism as the means of salvation or to preach the resurrection. In trying so hard to find alternative meanings to the Scriptures, the obvious truth is lost. We are baptized by the blood of Christ into His death, meaning that *we are not who we used to be* and since that happened, we now live our lives "through Jesus Christ our Lord."

Believer, you should learn to view the finished work of Christ as the epitome of the Great Exchange. See everything that Jesus went through as having been done for you. If He did it, and it is truly finished, what more could you add to make it "more finished"? The very term "more finished" doesn't even make sense! Who do we think we are that there is something we could do to finish what Jesus has already finished?

The following is a list of things Jesus took so that you could get the opposite. It could be better said that Jesus took what you deserved so that you could have what He earned. Notice that you have not earned any of the good things, for salvation comes only by faith, not by works (Ephesians 2:8, 9). This list is not conclusive, as grace is always showing us more of what Jesus paid for.

- Jesus was made to be sin, so that you could be made the righteousness of God (2 Corinthians 5:21).

- Jesus was naked at the cross so that you could be clothed in robes of righteousness (John 19:23; Luke 15:22).

- Jesus was made poor so that you could be made rich (2 Corinthians 8:9).

- Jesus was cursed so that you would be blessed (Galatians 3:13, 14).

- Jesus died in the dark so that you could live in the light (Matthew 27:45).

- Jesus cried, "My God, My God, why hast thou forsaken me?" so that you could cry, "Daddy, Daddy, why are you so good to me?" (Matthew 27:46; Romans 8:15).

- Jesus bore the crown of thorns, which represent the cares of this life (Matthew 13:22), so that the cares of this life would never trouble your mind.

- Jesus had His heart pierced so that your heart would never be broken again (John 19:34).

- Jesus drank the sour wine so that your teeth would never be set on edge (John 19:30; Ezekiel 18:1–3).

- Jesus' body was broken so that yours could always be whole (Matthew 26:26).

- Jesus was disciplined of His Father so that you could always be at peace with the Father (Isaiah 53:5).

- Jesus bore the full brunt of God's judgment against sin so that you would never bear any of God's judgment against sin (John 3:36; John 12:31, 32).

- Jesus defeated the devil so that you would never have to fight him (Hebrews 2:14).

- He sweat great drops of blood so that you would be freed from the curse of working for your spiritual bread.

The list could go on and on but I hope you get the point. Jesus did it all so that we get it all!

Because of the exchange, we have been reconciled. Remember the verse that we read earlier? Romans 5:10 says, "For if when we were enemies we were reconciled to God through the death of His Son, much more, having been reconciled, we shall be saved by His life." Christ's death at the cross has reconciled the world back to the Father, effectively removing the barrier that resulted from man's sin and rebellion. This means that there is nothing holding you back from receiving eternal life through Jesus Christ. When you receive, you are saved from day to day by Him living His life through you.

"Wait a minute, are you preaching some form of Universal Salvation, where everyone is saved right now, no matter what?"

Great question! If you had that question form in your head as you have been reading this chapter, I compliment you on being an astute guardian of the true message of grace. While we will explore grace in full detail throughout this book, this chapter discusses how God's grace brings about a great exchange: our lives for His. It is called grace because the exchange is absolutely free.

Just because grace is free does not mean that it is functioning fully in the heart and life of every human being. This is because, as awesome and wonderful as God's grace is, there is still the need for an activator in order for it to go to work in our hearts. The activator for grace is our faith, without which, "it is impossible to please Him" (Hebrews 11:6). Nothing pleases God more than His beloved Jesus, of whom He said that He was, "well pleased" (Matthew 3:17). If Jesus pleases God, our faith in Jesus and acceptance of His price paid for us is well pleasing to the Father as well. When our faith is placed in the finished work of Christ, God graces us with the exchanged life, simply on the basis of our faith.

Universal Salvation teaches that all men are saved because of the death of Christ on the cross, whether they ever acknowledge it or not. They contend that men are born lost, with no works of their own. Thus, the finished work at the cross makes them saved with no works of their own. This is true as it regards works, but God doesn't call faith and works by the same name. In fact, faith and works are polar opposites. God doesn't consider your acceptance of Jesus by faith as a work, simply as an acknowledgment of the price paid for your sins. Paul stated the case for faith as the grace activator this way:

> "For by grace you have been saved through faith, and that not of yourselves; it is the gift of God, not of works, lest anyone should boast" (Ephesians 2:8, 9).

Do you see how simple faith in Christ's finished work puts His righteousness into you so that you can show forth His life? Now that you are a believer, you are a, "new creation" (2 Corinthians 5:17), with all of your old sins and troubles having passed away.

With faith as the activator to God's grace operating in our lives, the responsibility to change falls on Christ within us. To maintain us in the midst of a changing world, the blood of Jesus Christ now goes to work to cleanse us from all that we used to be. Paul's letter to Romans gives us insight into how God's war against sin is over, and we are partakers through faith:

> "Therefore, having been justified by faith, we have peace with God through our Lord Jesus Christ" (Romans 5:1).

This justification is our salvation, which happened because of faith. Now that we are saved, watch what happens, within the same chapter, to keep us in that peace with God:

> "Much more then, having now been justified by His blood, we shall be saved from wrath through Him" (Romans 5:9).

Now that we are saved, our day-to-day lives are preserved not by our perfect faith but by His perfect blood. In other words, even when your faith waivers, His blood is constant!

Good point! Think of it this way: when the children of Israel marked the doors of their homes with the blood of a spotless lamb, they were doing it in response to God's promise that "When I see the blood, I will pass over you" (Exodus 12:13). God's final plague on Egypt was to be the death of the firstborn of all of the land, with only the blood on the door holding back that judgment. The act of placing the blood on the door was one of faith, as you believed it would spare you from God's wrath.

Once inside the house, your faith could wane, and you could even begin to doubt. For instance, the family members might say, "I don't know if this blood thing is going to work or not!" With that kind of attitude, do you suppose the blood would work? If your answer is no, you think that the blood's effectiveness is contingent on your attitude. If your answer is, "Yes, the blood must work," you can see that once the blood is placed on the door, it is the blood that makes the difference.

The blood of Jesus Christ, shed on the cross, is the atonement for you and me. Paul said that through our Lord Jesus Christ, we have received, "the atonement" (Romans 5:11). The New Testament was written in Greek, and the word used for "atonement" here was the Greek word *katalaga,* which means "exchange." Paul is stating that because of the blood of the finished work, we have received the great exchange: His life for ours!

"So Pastor, do you think that people can just accept Jesus and then never change, and they are all right?"

I think the question is uninformed. You can no more accept Jesus and never change than you can jump in the water and not get wet! Arguing over whether people have accepted Christ based on the things in their lives is to miss the point of God's exchange program. He is slowly but surely living His life through us. Granted, not all of the fruits of His righteousness will bud out at the same time, but they will most assuredly come.

"But aren't we supposed to be 'fruit inspectors'? Didn't Jesus say that you will know a tree by its fruit?"

Jesus did not say that you will know a tree by its fruit; but He did say that you will, "know them by their fruits" (Matthew 7:16). It is important to know who the "them" are to which He refers. To find it, simply backtrack one verse: "Beware of false prophets, who come to you in sheep's clothing, but inwardly they are ravenous wolves." The "them" of verse 16 refers to false prophets who have come to destroy God's flock. In light of this, our job as "fruit inspectors" is to make sure the voices that are teaching us are leading us to fruit production and not on to more works of the flesh.

When the Apostle Paul dealt with sin in the church at Corinth, he felt it necessary to remind the Corinthian Christians that they were not unrighteous, though they used to be. Even though there are incidents of incest, fornication, frivolous lawsuits, and drunkenness in the church at Corinth, Paul points the Corinthian believers away from what they used to be and on to what they have become.

> "And such were some of you. But you were washed, but you were sanctified, but you were justified in the name of the Lord Jesus and by the Spirit of our God" (1 Corinthians 6:11).

The evidence does not all point to an exchanged life ... yet. However, Paul knows that they are believers, as he personally led many of them to Christ. He knows that they have been washed of their sins, sanctified for God's use, and justified by the precious blood of Jesus.

This chapter has been intended to show you how God has designed to transform you without the interference of your efforts. I have endeavored to instill in you the blessed assurance that our Father is found in relationship, not in religion. Religion has no converts without radicalism or cults, and these survive on fear and intimidation. May you have no fear and feel no intimidation as you look into the glorious light of our Lord Jesus Christ.

Jesus told the Pharisees that God preferred mercy and not sacrifice (Matthew 9:13). Mercy is what you extend to those you love (relationship), while sacrifice is what you offer to the one you want to please (religion). If God preferred relationship to religion, do you think that He has changed His heart now?

You remember where you came from and know where you want to be, but where you are can be frustrating and discouraging. As you read the following chapters, let the grace of our lovely Jesus transform you into His image. See the Great Exchange as having already started in your heart and life, and prepare yourself for some powerful truths. I am excited about what He is going to reveal to you and do in you. Are you ready? Let's go!

God's Justice System | 3

The previous chapter explained God's exchange system: Jesus was made to be sin so that we could be made the righteousness of God. I promised to deal with the judgment side of that system in more detail in this chapter, so let's begin with an important statement that gets the ball rolling toward understanding God's system of justice in dealing with mankind.

Since our sins have been punished in the body of Jesus, God's righteousness is on our side, demanding our acquittal.

Stop and reread that sentence one more time. Let it soak in. Do you believe it? Can you accept that all of your sins have been punished in the body of Jesus? Further, can you accept that God's righteousness is on your side now, insisting that the price has been paid, freeing you from the obligation of repayment? If this statement is hard to swallow, it could be because there are a couple of words that need further explanation. As the terminology is understood, I believe that the power of the statement will begin to be clear.

First, let's get an understanding of what "righteousness" is all about. The first time that we see the word used in the Bible is way back in Genesis, when we find that Abraham believed in the Lord and that his faith was "counted to him for righteousness" (Genesis 15:6 KJV). Since the Old Testament was written in Hebrew and the New Testament was written in Greek, we will often refer to the meaning of a particular word as it was used in that original language. In this case, the Hebrew word for "righteousness" means "rectitude, right, or justice," showing us that Abraham was considered "right" in the eyes of God simply by faith. Using that definition, God's righteousness demanding our acquittal would mean that God's justice demands that we go free simply based on our faith in the finished work of Jesus.

Righteousness is essentially the theme of the New Testament, with the word appearing therein some ninety-two times. The author of the New Covenant, the Apostle Paul, uses it thirty times in the book of Romans alone! *Strong's Online Concordance* defines "righteousness" this way: "In a broad sense: the state of him who is as he ought to be; the condition acceptable to God."

Now that we know what righteousness is, and we understand that we have been declared righteous by faith because of Christ's finished work, let's find out why God's righteousness within us demands our acquittal. Since our sin was punished in Jesus, a righteous God can only remain righteous by *not* punishing those sins in us. This is the very reason why you and I have been acquitted from all guilt and condemnation. In essence, God cannot be mad at us, because He was already mad at Jesus!

I used to say from the pulpit, "Don't ask God for justice, ask God for mercy!" I thought that I was being quite profound, as I was pointing out that God's justice should fry you in hell for all that you had done wrong. I was under the impression that Calvary was God being merciful toward man, though we deserved no mercy. Without realizing what I was doing, I was devaluing the blood of Christ by making His payment a whitewashing, rather than a cleansing, of our sins. By saying that God's justice will judge man, we are saying that the cross of Christ was not enough judgment against sin and that God did not exhaust His anger at Calvary. In a nutshell, we do not view God as having sufficiently punished our sins in the body of Jesus; therefore, we are convinced that He must judge them in us.

The Apostle Paul said that Jesus Christ was made unto us righteousness (1 Corinthians 1:30). This means that Jesus in us has made us perfectly righteous. This cannot be if there is sin left to be judged, for that sin would negate God's righteousness through Christ. We must begin to see the cross as either a finished work or an unfinished work. There can be no in-between.

> **"Pastor, I accept that Jesus bore my sins, but how can I be acquitted? I mean, I know that I still do things that are wrong. Shouldn't I expect to be punished in some way for my failures?"**

That is a common question, because it is a universal thought. Since God is the ultimate judge of all mankind, it is easy to assume that He is in heaven with a big ledger, marking down all of our rights and wrongs. This idea, however, gives no respect to what Jesus paid for, and it ignores how horrendous and beautiful that the cross truly was.

To properly answer this question, let's take an amazing journey back to the Garden to see an event that set a tone for how God would deal with both mankind and our sin.

In Bible study, there is a technique used to understand topics and context called the Law of First Mention. This rule of study states that the first time that a word is used in the Bible sets the tone for how it can be interpreted throughout the Word of God. For instance, the first time that the word "grace" is used is in Genesis 6:8: "But Noah found grace in the eyes of the Lord." In Hebrew, "Noah" means "rest," thus, "Rest finds grace." Throughout the Bible, you will find that grace and rest are linked due to the Law of First Mention.

The first time that the word "sword" is used occurs just after God has kicked Adam and Eve out of the Garden. In order to keep the couple from eating from the Tree of Life and living forever in their fallen state, God sends them out of the Garden and assigns angels to guard the tree with, "a flaming sword which turned every way, to guard the way to the Tree of Life" (Genesis 3:24). The sword was designed to cut and punish anyone who dared touch the fruit from this most sacred tree. Without redemption, man's sins barred him from access to eternal life, and the sword of God's judgment carried out the sentence.

Distance from man was never God's will. Sin had become the great barrier to relationship, which God longed to have with His prize creation. Remember, when God created the heavens, the earth, and the animals, He said that it was "good." But when He made man, He declared him to be "very good" (Genesis 1:31). The heart of God longed for mankind to eat of the fruits of eternal life and righteousness, but His anger at sin was too great, and the sword of judgment stood as a stark barrier to intimacy.

Fast-forward a few thousand years to the time of the prophet Zechariah. Like all Old Testament prophets, Zechariah saw the future like the tops of a distant mountain range; he knew what was coming, but he couldn't tell which event was first, second, or last. This is the reason that within one verse of prophecy you might see two different periods of time. It takes the passage of that time and the anointing of the Holy Spirit to determine when and where these scriptures find their fulfillment.

"And one shall say unto Him, 'What are these wounds in thine hands?' Then He shall answer, 'Those with which I was wounded in the house of my friends'" (Zechariah 13:6 KJV).

It's pretty easy to figure out where and how Jesus received the wounds in His hands, isn't it? We know that He was pierced at the cross. This knowledge helps us connect the dots for when we read the next verse:

"Awake, O sword, against my shepherd, and against the man that is my fellow, saith the Lord of hosts: smite the shepherd, and the sheep shall be scattered" (Zechariah 13:7 KJV).

This verse marks the last time that the word "sword" is used in the Old Testament. Remember that the Law of First Mention taught us that "sword" has come to stand for God's judgment and separation of man from eternal life. Asleep outside the Garden, the sword of judgment is now being called to wake up and "smite the shepherd." God's anger has obviously been aroused, and His sword of judgment is about to drink someone's blood!

This sword belongs to God, and He reserves the right to use it wherever and upon whomever He chooses. He has had it resting outside of Eden to keep man from eternal life, but as we explained, this doesn't line up with His heart, for He longs to relate with mankind. Though He loves man very much, He is so righteous that the sin of man stinks in His nostrils. The very creation of a sword of anger and judgment came about to make someone pay for that stench. The Psalmist said of God's anger and His weaponry:

"God judgeth the righteous, and God is angry every day. If He turn not, He will whet His sword; He hath bent His bow, and made it ready. He hath also prepared for Him the instruments of death; He ordaineth His arrows against the persecutors" (Psalm 7:11–13 KJV).

I intentionally left out the words "with the wicked," which the King James Version uses to describe who God is angry with "every day." I did so because if you will notice, those words are italicized in the King James, meaning that they were added by the translators. In truth, under the Old Covenant, God was not just angry with the wicked, He was just angry in general. Without something to appease Him, "He will whet His sword." To which sword do you suppose this refers?

The sword is being told to wake up to strike one specific individual. This person is described as "my shepherd" and "my fellow." The Hebrew word used here for "fellow" is the same word used for "relation," indicating that the sword is to smite someone closely related to God. Watch Jesus describe Himself in very similar terms:

> "I am the good shepherd. The good shepherd gives His life for the sheep" (John 10:11).

> "I am the good shepherd; and I know My sheep, and am known by My own. As the Father knows Me, even so I know the Father; and I lay down My life for the sheep" (John 10:14, 15).

What a wonderful connection! Jesus describes Himself as the good shepherd, and He relates Himself to the Father. Both descriptions fit the recipient of the sword from Zechariah 13.

"That's an interesting connection, but how can we be sure that Zechariah was talking about Jesus' death on the cross?"

When I first saw Zechariah's prophecy, I wondered the same thing. Though the verse is linked to the one in front of it, in which Jesus' hands are pierced, making the connection between the sword and the shepherd as being God's judgment placed in Jesus seemed like it might be a stretch; that is, until I found out that Jesus made the same connection.

On the night before He went to the cross, Jesus and the disciples shared a meal, sang a hymn, and then departed for the Mount of Olives. Here, Jesus quotes an Old Testament passage to warn the disciples not only of His impending death but of their denial of Him as their Savior. I'll highlight the portion of the verse that should look very familiar by now:

> "Then saith Jesus unto them, 'All ye shall be offended because of me this night: for it is written, *I will smite the shepherd, and the sheep of the flock shall be scattered abroad*'" (Matthew 26:31 KJV).

Jesus is quoting our passage from Zechariah to show His disciples that He is the shepherd! Now, let's put two and two together, so to speak. If Jesus declares Himself to be the shepherd of Zechariah's prophecy, and He knows that He is about to die on the cross, doesn't it make sense that the sword of that prophecy is waking up to kill Jesus?

Since the sword is representative of God's anger and judgment and is to smite the shepherd (Jesus), we must decide whether it is biblical to declare that God killed His own Son. Of course, most Christians would nod their head in approval that God offered up Jesus for us, but many feel that the Romans or the Jews actually killed Jesus and that this just served God's purpose. I propose to you that no man killed Jesus, because Jesus Himself told us, "'I lay down my life, that I might take it again. No man taketh it from me, but I lay it down of myself'" (John 10:17, 18 KJV).

While Jesus had to offer up His life willingly as a sacrifice for sins, the punishment and pain He endured prior to that offering was placed on Him by the very hand of God the Father. Isaiah said that Jesus was, "smitten by God, and afflicted," and that "it pleased the Lord to bruise Him" (Isaiah 53:4, 10). He also wrote that the Father would see the travail of Jesus on the cross and that He would be satisfied (Isaiah 53:11).

Why would God do this to His own Son? How could smiting Jesus bring God any pleasure? Didn't He love Jesus? The answer to all of these questions is summed up in one statement: God loves you and me so much that it pleased Him to punish our sins in Jesus so that He would not have to punish them in us. Hallelujah!

Not only did Jesus view Himself as the smitten shepherd, He also knew that the smiting was God's judgment against all sin and that He was the recipient of all God's wrath. To the man He had healed of blindness, Jesus said, "'For judgment I have come into this world, that those who do not see may see, and that those who see may be made blind'" (John 9:39). He knew He was here to be judged so that all who thought they were righteous by their works would know better, and all who were spiritually blind could be made to see.

Jesus spoke of God's judgment again in John 12:32, when He said, "'And I, if I be lifted up from the earth, will draw all unto me.'" Does that verse look unusual? Again, I dropped an italicized word from the text, because it did not appear in the original Greek. The word "men," or "peoples," was added by the translators to try to explain that if Jesus is lifted up, everyone will be drawn to Him. Without that word, this verse needs the verse in front of it to show us exactly what Jesus is going to draw into Himself on the cross:

> "'Now is the judgment of this world: now shall the prince of this world be cast out. And I, if I be lifted up from the earth, will draw all unto me'" (John 12:31, 32 KJV).

Jesus is telling us that He will be lifted up on a cross, and this very act will draw all of the judgment that is aimed at the world into Him. What an amazing statement! God's wrath and anger, typified by His sword of judgment, was plunged into Jesus at the cross, making Jesus the resting place for God's "instruments of death" (Psalm 7:13).

Remember, this judgment against our sins in the body of Jesus could not have been possible if Jesus had not been sinless in His own life and if He had not bore our sins willingly. The pain of God's judgment was to be so severe that in Gethsemane, Jesus prayed, "'O My Father, if it is possible, let this cup pass from Me; nevertheless, not as I will, but as You will'" (Matthew 26:39). He was not asking to avoid the cross because of the beating, the crown of thorns, or the nails; He was asking because He dreaded the wrath of the Father being poured into Him.

In the Old Testament, anyone who had committed a sin was to bring a spotless lamb to the tabernacle as atonement for his sins. The priest would examine the lamb to ensure that it was worthy. Then, the sinner would lay his hands on the head of the animal as a symbol of the transference of his sins into its body. The lamb would then be killed in place of the man, effectively freeing the man from his guilt. This system was symbolic only, as the blood of the animals could never truly take away sin from the heart (Hebrews 10:4).

Jesus was the Lamb of God, who came to take away the sin of the world (John 1:29). God inspected Him for sin and failure and found none. God then transferred all of our sins into Him so that we could be freed from our guilt and condemnation. This act was *not* symbolic, as the blood of Jesus can and does take sin away from our heart (Hebrews 10:10, 12).

Having seen a little glimpse of the sacrificial system of atonement, and understanding how significant that Jesus' death at Calvary was, let's look for a moment at the cross itself to find more fantastic truths about our redemption.

The book of Mark tells us that Jesus was crucified at the third hour of the day. The Jewish way of keeping time was to start the daily clock at 6 a.m., meaning that the third hour of the day would have been sometime around 9 a.m. Three of the Gospels then explain that there was darkness over all the land from the sixth hour through the ninth hour, meaning that from noon until 3 p.m., Jesus suffered under the cover of midday darkness.

Under Mosaic Law, the priests in the temple were to offer two daily sacrifices for the people of Israel. One was considered the morning sacrifice, and the other was the evening sacrifice. Would you like to venture a guess as to what time these were to occur? The morning sacrifice was offered at 9 a.m., and the evening sacrifice was offered at 3 p.m., corresponding with the time Jesus went on the cross and when He ultimately died.

Notice that the sacrificial system came first, long before the cross. God must have had Calvary in mind way back in the Old Testament, as He designed the system of sacrifice to be built around the future sacrifice of His only Son. What forethought!

During this time of darkness, Jesus endured the punishment and the pain for all of our sicknesses and disease, causing Him to cry out, "'My God, My God, why have You forsaken Me?'" (Matthew 27:46). This is the only recorded time in Jesus' ministry that He calls His Father, "God." Our sins in His body had caused the Father to turn away from Jesus, separating the two of them from the unity that Jesus had always enjoyed. Even in His own Son, God's hatred for sin was too great to ignore. Jesus suffered through this time of darkness so that you and I could live in the light!

I was recently dwelling on this particular moment at Calvary, just feeding my soul on the wonderful things that Jesus had accomplished for me at the cross, when I noticed something incredible. God split the time that His Son spent on the cross right down the middle. Jesus hung in the light for three hours and then He suffered in the dark for three hours. I saw it as God giving exactly the same amount of judgment to Jesus as He had given Him light. My soul was settled with the news that God made sure all of my sins were paid for by punishing every one of them in the body of Jesus. Punishment for sin, split down the middle; nothing was left undone.

The longer I dwelled on that revelation, though, the more something bothered me. I have grown to believe that God's grace is not only sufficient for all of my sins but that His grace is greater than my sins. In fact, Paul said as much in Romans 5:20: "Where sin abounded, grace abounded much more." I began to question the Lord on why the time spent in the dark was only equal to the time spent in the light. Shouldn't Jesus have spent slightly more time in the dark so that grace would be made to abound in me?

The gentle voice of the Spirit showed me Jesus suffering in Gethsemane, known in the Greek as "the place of the olive press." Sufficiently crushed, Jesus goes on to the mockery and shame of Pilate's Hall, where He is stripped naked, whipped, beaten, and then crowned with thorns. Finally, His hands and feet are pierced, and He is hoisted high above the ground to endure the verbal abuse of the riotous crowd. Only then did I begin to see that long before the sky grew black, my Jesus had already done enough to pay for my sins and my sicknesses. The darkness at Calvary was not God's way of equaling the score; it was God's way of going farther than was necessary. In other words, the darkness was God's *overpayment* for our sins.

You can rest in the assurance that Jesus has borne your sicknesses and carried your sorrows. He was so marred at Calvary that men turned their faces from what they saw. I believe that this occurred during those three horrific hours, when Jesus took every cancer and tumor and disease that would ever strike humanity and had them punished in His body. Don't just see Jesus as having carried them; see God as having judged them in Jesus, freeing you from the fear that God is looking to judge them in you.

Since Jesus bore all condemnation in His flesh, there is none left for you. Paul said that God "condemned sin in the flesh," meaning that all sin has been sufficiently condemned in Jesus. Because of this, "There is therefore now no condemnation to those who are in Christ Jesus" (Romans 8:1).

"There is a qualifier for no condemnation, Pastor. The rest of Romans 8:1 tells us that we are not condemned if we walk after the Spirit."

Actually, if you study Greek scholars, and even many reference Bibles, you will find that the last phrase of Romans 8:1 is an interpolated Scripture, meaning that it did not appear in the original text and that translators moved it from one spot to another to further the understanding of the verse. In this case, the translators took a portion of Romans 8:4 and moved it to the end of Romans 8:1, because even they had a hard time believing that God's gift of no condemnation came with no qualifier other than being "in Christ Jesus." Whether they accepted it or not, Paul's words ring true, and you can rejoice in them: there is now no condemnation!

Perhaps we can get an even better understanding if we remember this simple fact: *God is not being merciful in not judging you for your sins; He is being righteous.* Mercy would indicate that you deserve punishment but that He simply chooses not to give it. That makes God less than holy. Instead, when God doesn't punish man for sins, He is maintaining His righteousness by being true to what He has already accomplished in Jesus.

> "To demonstrate at the present time His righteousness, that He might be just and the justifier of the one who has faith in Jesus" (Romans 3:26).

Paul felt that God could only be considered just if He justifies you based purely on your faith in Jesus. This message brings back the honor and glory to the finished work of the cross and pulls all glory away from man's efforts. That was the design of relationship in the first place.

Since the price had been paid through the suffering of the darkness, God turned His face back toward His Son just before Christ's death. Jesus called Him "Father" again (Luke 23:46), meaning that fellowship had been restored between Father and Son. Then He cried, "'It is finished'" (John 19:30). Never forget, "It is finished," means that God's war against sin is over, because the sword of fury and anger has been silenced in Jesus.

"Pastor Paul, all of this teaching about sin being judged is going to make people believe that sin is no big deal. It sounds like you don't take sin very seriously!"

I disagree! I take sin very seriously, and so does God. In fact, He took it so seriously that He went to all of this trouble to punish it in the body of Jesus. It could be argued that if you are always dwelling on sin and punishment, you don't take the cross of Christ very seriously.

Now that you know that the judgment of God rested in the body of Jesus, there should be no judgment left for you to throw out at those around you. Jesus told Peter in Gethsemane that those who take the sword shall perish with the sword and that he should put it away (Matthew 26:52). Doling out judgment on others shows you have yet to accept that Jesus was judged for you. Put away your sword of anger and judgment, and show others that God has done the same.

Later in this book, we will deal in detail with the difference in the judgment of unbelievers versus the judgment of believers. For now, let's keep our hearts and minds focused on God's system of justice and how it revolves around the price paid by Jesus. When our focus shifts from the finished work it goes onto unfinished man. This causes us to sharpen our sword and come down with harshness on those around us. Jesus said that we will be judged by what judgment we use (Matthew 7:1). Don't you want your judgment to be based on what Christ has done for you?

Go back over the principles in this chapter again and again if necessary. Read it until the revelation of God's judgment of all of your sins in the body of Christ becomes a part of your Christian walk. The Holy Spirit inside of you is working even right now to make you free from the old law of sin and death (Romans 8:2), and the knowledge that you are not condemned for those sins is a crucial first step in allowing Christ to transform you into His image.

The Need for Another Awakening | 4

As a father of two, I find that I must occasionally shout, "Wake up!" to my children when they seem a bit lazy getting out of bed on a school morning. Every parent knows what I'm talking about, and every child loathes hearing those words. They want to stay in bed, because they are sleepy from staying up too late the night before or because the bed is just so comfortable. The problem is that they need to get up and get ready for school, and they can't accomplish these things if they are lying in bed.

There seems to be a spiritual cry of "Wake up!" coming from churches and pulpits in an ever-increasing volume. There is talk of another "Great Awakening," with messages hearkening back to the previous awakenings in American history that sparked a renewed religious fervor and consecration. This thought is the inspiration for revivals, seminars, conferences, and concerts as ministries regenerate a new level of morality and dedication from believers they claim will be the catalyst for a move of God unlike the world has ever seen.

Let me state from the outset of this chapter that I agree we need another awakening. We desperately need to wake up to a truth that has been covered up and slandered. However, the renewal of a Great Awakening that is being touted by many, which demands a high level of morality in order to be blessed, or increased consecration in order to have a move of God is not only not the answer but is actually the very opposite of what the church needs!

Before I go any further, let me show you an almost forgotten statement by the Apostle Paul that should be the springboard Scripture for a new awakening:

"Awake to righteousness, and sin not" (1 Corinthians 15:34, KJV).

Good.

① Paul agreed that there needed to be an awakening within the body of Christ, one in which the believer wakes up to how righteous he is in God through the finished work of Christ. He believed when saints wake up to the simple fact that they are righteous apart from their works, they will be empowered to "sin not." This little verse holds important truths in our quest to transform the way that we live and act, because it contains the formula for living free from the dominion of sin: "Awake to righteousness!"

Now, let's go back to our previous statement that the modern message of Great Awakening is the opposite of what the church needs. How can we say that when the idea of an awakening speaks so highly of consecration, fasting, giving, working, and witnessing? Let's answer that in light of what we have already learned about the finished work of Jesus Christ.

Remember that the cross of Christ is where God put all of our sins into the body of Jesus and then judged them there. This frees us from the curse of sin and allows us to freely receive of God's blessings. In fact, Paul said that God has, "blessed us with every spiritual blessing in the heavenly places in Christ" (Ephesians 1:3). Our blessings come upon us, "in Christ," and not as a result of our works. The phrase "in Christ" speaks of what Jesus accomplished at the cross when He became sin for all of us.

Since our blessings come because Jesus dwells in us, there can be no blessing that comes upon us due to increasing our level of consecration or cleaning up certain areas of our lives. If God responded to our actions by giving us blessings when we are good and judgment when we aren't so good, He would be rewarding us based on our work instead of based on Jesus' finished work.

When the church hears the message that it should clean up so God will bless it, it is hearing that God's favor and goodwill come only when it is deserving of them. It is also being taught that God is holding back blessings from it because it is not "living up" to some standard. Do you see how this completely removes the finished work of Christ from our sights? Paul said it this way:

> "Now to him who works, the wages are not counted as grace but as debt. But to him who does not work but believes on Him who justifies the ungodly, his faith is accounted for righteousness" (Romans 4:4, 5).

Our righteousness is in no way affected by whether or not we work for it. In fact, that which we receive because we worked for it cannot be called God's grace but, rather, God's payment. In effect, when we think increased prayer time, fasting, giving, and consecration will get God's attention and cause Him to pour out blessings and revival, we believe that God actually owes us goodness. This makes our idea of a Great Awakening a prepayment to God for all of His mercy and grace. How absurd!

I have heard it said that great revival will only come to America when the church of Jesus Christ wakes up from its slumber and begins to pray and repent. The same message states that the level to which we pray will determine the level to which we awake, and the level to which we awake will determine the magnitude of God's judgment against us. Do you realize what this is saying? This kind of doctrine ignores the cross of Christ, effectively declaring that man's actions, and not the finished work of Jesus, determines how God deals with us.

Whether we realize it or not, this wake-up message, which is being packaged as a modern-day renewal, is one of works and self-effort. It is subtly creating a hybrid religion of Christian principles with Jewish customs and laws. While boasting of being a New Covenant people, we are slowly but surely acting as if the cross never happened, going so far as to place heavy emphasis on Jewish feast days, kosher foods, and prayer shawls. Oftentimes, in an attempt to get closer to God, we distance ourselves from the one thing that moves His heart the most: the finished work of His Son at Calvary.

I firmly believe that we need to wake up. In fact, I believe it so much that it is one of the primary reasons I have written this book. It should be shouted from the housetops that Jesus was made to be sin so that we could be made the righteousness of God in Christ. The sooner we wake up to that fact, the sooner we will accomplish great things for God in this darkened world.

One of our chief responsibilities as children of God is the spreading of light to a dark world. In these final hours, more than ever, saints need to shine as light and flavor as salt a world that is in the dark and has no flavor. To do this, we must wake up to who we are in Christ. When you fall asleep as to how God views you, you fall back into the habits that you formed when you were living for the world. This is why we see some believers doing things that we know believers shouldn't be doing. It is not that they are lost; it is that they have simply fallen asleep on how righteous they are in Christ.

"Pastor, I'm sorry, but there is no way that I am going to say to someone who has an obvious problem with sin, 'You just need to wake up to your righteousness in Jesus'! That just won't work."

I added that statement, because I have had that argument used against me regarding the message of righteousness. Some people have a hard time with the idea that we are righteous in God due to the finished work of Christ—even when all of our actions are not righteous. If we fall asleep on that righteousness, it stands to reason that the fruits of righteousness cannot and will not spring forth from our life. Therefore, believers who live below the standard of God's righteousness are simply asleep to whom they are in Christ. Someone needs to get radical about grace and wake them up!

Satan deals better with a sleeping saint than he does with one who is awake. It has been this way from the beginning, as Satan found early on that it is easier to deceive mankind if you can get him to deny that he is righteous through works other than his own.

In chapter 2, we said that Eve ate the fruit to be more righteous, not to be rebellious. Satan tempted her on the grounds that there was more righteousness to be had by something that *she could do*. In her desire to be more righteous, she fell for the bait. Satan was preaching a form of awakening to her, trying to "wake her up" to the fact there was something more that she didn't have. What he was really doing was lulling her to sleep to the truth that she was already righteous.

How does Satan get the saint to fall into a slumber now? The common answers are, "He gets us to sin," and, "He makes us apathetic." These answers are given so often most believers don't even question them. Instead, they just nod in approval. But is this how Satan gets us to go to sleep?

Paul addressed the issue of justification coming by faith and not by law in his writing to the church at Galatia. He stated that if righteousness came by the law, "then Christ died in vain" (Galatians 2:21), meaning that if we could be righteous through the keeping of the law, Christ died for no reason. He continues his train of thought into the next chapter, when he asks an important question:

> O foolish Galatians! Who has bewitched you that you should not obey the truth, before whose eyes Jesus Christ was clearly portrayed among you as crucified? This only I want to learn from you: Did you receive the Spirit by the works of the law, or by the hearing of faith? Are you so foolish? Having begun in the Spirit, are you now being made perfect by the flesh?" (Galatians 3:1–3).

The word "bewitched" is translated from the Greek word *baskaino*, which means "hypnotized." Paul is asking the Galatian Christians who hypnotized them into believing that they were saved by the power of the Holy Spirit, but they can only go on unto perfection through the flesh. Within context of these verses, Paul's usage of flesh points to their inability to keep the law through their works or self-efforts.

Not only does Paul see them as having been hypnotized, he also calls them "foolish," something he never does to any of his other churches. The Greek word used here is *anoetos*, and it means "stupidity that arises from deadness." Does Paul believe that these believers are dead? Of course not! However, he does believe they have been hypnotized into a state of deadness, convinced there is something more they need to do in order to be considered righteous in the eyes of God.

This looks like the work of Satan, doesn't it? His fingerprints are all over this blueprint. Just as he bewitched Eve in the Garden of Eden and caused her to go to sleep on how righteous she already was, he had done the same thing to the church at Galatia. His work of putting the church to sleep is not now, nor has it ever been, to get believers to fall into sin. *Satan's greatest work against the church of Jesus Christ is to hypnotize us with self-righteousness and man-made efforts at religion, causing us to fall asleep to how righteous we are in Christ.*

I must admit that this parallel we are making between Satan's temptation of Eve in Eden and the lulling to sleep of the church is not original. The Apostle Paul made the parallel long before I did:

"But I fear, lest somehow, as the serpent deceived Eve by his craftiness, so your minds may be corrupted from the simplicity that is in Christ" (2 Corinthians 11:3).

Paul gave the warning of Satan's devices to the believers at Corinth, fearing that their minds would be taken away from dwelling on just how simple Christ is. This is not insinuating that Jesus is a simpleton, but rather that salvation is so simple due to the fact that Jesus has already done all of the work at the cross!

This phenomenon of sleeping saints is not a new problem. As we have seen, Paul had to deal with it happening in his day. He told the church at Rome the same thing when he said, "And do this, knowing the time, that now it is high time to awake out of sleep; for now our salvation is nearer than when we first believed (Romans 13:11). And to the church at Ephesus, he repeated the warning with, "Awake, you who sleep, arise from the dead, and Christ will give you light" (Ephesians 5:14). Again, he is speaking to believers who are falling asleep as to who they are in Christ.

The danger of living our Christian lives in a state of slumber is that we are constantly susceptible to the attacks of the enemy. Those who sleep are naturally to do so at night, when it is dark. Those who are awake are aided by the light of the sun, which shines forth during the day. Paul told believers that they used to be darkness, "but now you are light in the Lord. Walk as children of light" (Ephesians 5:8). To slumber and sleep now that we have the light of Christ shining in our lives is to live in much the same manner as those who are dwelling in the darkness.

We have all heard that sinning will cause us to slumber in our Christian walk, but in light of what you and I have just discovered in God's word, that statement should be reconsidered. We should not say that sin leads to slumber but that *slumber leads to sin*. This is precisely why we should, "Awake to righteousness and sin not."

Throughout the Bible, there are examples of how slumber can lead to problems in people's lives. Satan has always taken advantage of the slumbering saint, starting with Noah. The builder of the Ark is a prime example of how slumber leads to sin. When he fell into a drunken stupor, His son Ham saw his nakedness and defiled his father. While living in a fresh, new world with heaven's rainbow in the sky, Noah fell asleep to who he was, and the next generation paid the price.

Samson rested his head in the lap of Delilah and had his seven locks of hair cut off. The number seven represents God's rest and perfection, as He rested from Creation on the seventh day. As soon as Samson fell asleep to the power of the covenant God had made with him, his rest was cut off, and failure was soon to follow.

In Gethsemane, while Jesus prayed to the Father, Peter, James, and John slept. They did not appreciate the importance of the moment, and their sleep preceded a wholesale denial on the part of the disciples.

I am not insinuating that physical sleep brings on the attack of the enemy, but I do believe that we have shown that falling asleep to the righteousness of God in our lives will open the door for the enemy to do damage. It is His righteousness in us that holds back the attacks of the enemy in the first place. Losing sight of His righteousness causes us to perform our own righteousness, making His finished work of no effect.

Remaining alert and awake to His righteousness in us should be the natural thing for us to do now that we are born again. As we studied in the previous chapter Jesus was cut off from the Father at Calvary so that we would never be cut off. Since our sins have been punished in the body of Jesus, we have His righteousness at work in us. Paul said that we have received the circumcision, "made without hands," and this causes us to, "put off the body of the sins of the flesh, by the circumcision of Christ" (Colossians 2:11). We are not made whole because the baby Jesus was circumcised; we are made whole because Jesus was "circumcised" from the Father, and now He lives in us. *cut off. !*

It is easy to stay awake to our right-standing in God, as long as we are alert to the fact that Jesus was cut off for us. The more that we feed on the glorious truth of the finished work of Jesus, the easier it is to be alert in Him. As soon as we drift from the acknowledgment that He was cut off for us, we go to work to try and pay God back for our sins and indiscretions. This hypnotism causes us to fall asleep to the great truth of the finished work, and before long, we are back into the old "sins of the flesh."

I was studying this topic several years ago, when the Lord led me to a fascinating revelation regarding sleeping saints. Having already immersed myself in the wonderful message of grace, my heart was tendered and prepared for the glorious truth He was about to reveal to me, and now I am excited to share it with you. I pray that we have tendered your heart to His righteousness in you as well. We'll start with another word study from the original Greek text.   *1st*

There are two Greek words for sleep that are used in the New Testament. One Greek word is *koimao*, which means "to fall asleep or to die." Notice that it can mean either literal sleep or death, and the only way that we can interpret, it is used within the context of the Scriptures surrounding it. For instance, the word is used to describe the death by stoning of the Apostle Stephen (Acts 7:60), and it is also used to describe the sleeping disciples in the Garden of Gethsemane (Luke 22:45). In both cases, the English word "sleep" is rendered from the Greek word "koimao."

The other Greek word for sleep is *katheudo*, which means "to fall asleep." This word is always translated as "sleep" in one form or the other and never insinuates death. For instance, "katheudo" is used to describe Jesus sleeping through the storm (Matthew 8:24) and is used by Jesus when He says of Jairus' daughter, "She is not dead, but sleepeth" (Matthew 9:24).

When Paul writes of the resurrection in 1 Thessalonians 4, he speaks of those who, "sleep in Jesus" (verse 14). He uses koimao, and we know he means that they are dead, because the next verse reads, "For this we say to you by the word of the Lord, that we who are alive and remain until the coming of the Lord will by no means precede those who are asleep." Can you see that, within context, "sleep" here must mean "death," as Paul contrasted it with those of us who are alive?

Good point!,

Paul furthers his sermon into the fifth chapter and makes this statement: "Therefore let us not sleep, as others do, but let us watch and be sober. For those who sleep, sleep at night, and those who get drunk are drunk at night" (verses 6 and 7). Here, "sleep" is "katheudo," meaning, "to fall asleep." Paul is warning us to stay awake as to who we are in Christ. While the previous chapter is speaking of death, this one is speaking of life.

It all comes to a head in the next two verses, as Paul explains that the church must be removed in order for God's wrath to be poured out. Look closely as he describes the kind of people who are going to be with Jesus:

> "For God did not appoint us to wrath, but to obtain salvation through our Lord Jesus Christ, who died for us, that whether we wake or sleep, we should live together with Him" (1 Thessalonians 5:9, 10).

I have heard these verses used many times to say that when Jesus comes back, He will take the believers who are in the grave with Him as well as those of us that are alive. Why would Paul say this twice, seeing how he already said it in chapter 4, verses 16 and 17? "Sleep" here is "katheudo," meaning "to fall asleep," and remember, it never means 'dead.' This is not a statement about Jesus taking us whether we are alive or dead; rather, it is a statement about Him taking us whether we are awake to our righteousness or not. Can you see how exciting this is?

This motivates me to wake up to who I am in Christ, but not because I am afraid if I am asleep to that knowledge that I will die and go to hell. I want to be awake to my righteousness, because I am a child of the day and not of the night (1 Thessalonians 5:5). I want my light to shine so brightly in a darkened world that men see my good works and glorify my Father in heaven (Matthew 5:16). I want to be so alert to who I am in Jesus that I live the abundant life, allowing Jesus to live through me. Don't you want to walk in that light?

Now please notice that Paul guarantees we have not been appointed to wrath (1 Thessalonians 5:9). The reason that we do not have an appointment with God's wrath is because He has already punished our sins in the body of Jesus, and we have accepted Christ as our Savior. Even the sinner has had his sins punished in the body of Jesus, but his refusal to accept Jesus by faith will eventually place him under the wrath of God. If you die without having accepted Christ as the payment for your sins, you are rejecting God.

God's payment for your sins. None of us can handle that kind of judgment, so let's thank God for Jesus!

"Pastor, don't you think that telling people that they can be a slumbering saint and still go to heaven will promote a lackadaisical attitude toward Christianity?"

No! In fact, it is the only message that keeps Christ and His finished work at the center of our attention. If your alertness and soberness are what get you to heaven, you do not need Jesus Christ and His finished work. The straightforward, unadulterated message of the finished work of Jesus is the most selfless message that can be preached or taught, because it places no focus on the believer and puts all of it onto Jesus.

Saint, please see how emphasis on His righteousness in you brings Jesus into a brighter light of loveliness. With the focus no longer on you but on His righteousness within you, you will wake up to greater things in the Father. It will be impossible for you to live a life of sin and failure, because your day-to-day concentration will be on how much Jesus has paid for you and how much your Father must love you. Lazy Christianity will never be the end result of a life concentrated on the righteousness of Jesus Christ.

"But didn't Jesus tell the story of the five foolish virgins who slept while the bridegroom tarried and then didn't have enough oil in their lamps for the wedding?"

That is good point! The story of the five wise and five foolish virgins is found in Matthew 25. Take time to read that story again, and notice in verse 5, while the bridegroom tarried, "they all slumbered and slept." It wasn't just the five foolish virgins who slept, but it was the five wise as well. Notice, however, that there was no reprimand on the five wise, simply on the five foolish. Why do you suppose that was?

The five foolish virgins were left behind because they had no oil in their lamps, not because they were asleep. In fact, more insight is gleaned from the bridegroom's answer to them in verse 12 when He says, *"I know you not."* These virgins are not believers, for their lamps were not full. This story doesn't prove that slumbering kills, but it does prove that if you fill your vessel and fall asleep, you will be no good to those around you who do not know your bridegroom. ❧

Good point!.

There are sinners asleep all around us who have no knowledge whatsoever of Christ and His finished work. The longer we remain asleep, the fewer opportunities we have of winning those unbelievers to Jesus.

There are also many saints who are sleeping on their righteousness. Perhaps, until recently, you have been slumbering as well. I am not referring to your actions or thoughts, but maybe you have been asleep concerning the great truth of Christ's righteousness within you due to the cross, and this may be leading you to bad actions and thoughts.

If you have been asleep to this great truth, "Wake up!" There is too much to be done to continue slumbering away the days while the Sun of Righteousness is shining in this world. He is not condemning you or belittling you: He simply desires to see you free from the chains and trappings that are holding you back.

Your Jesus is so lovely and perfect within you, and He is still pleasing to the Father. John said, "As He is, so are we in this world" (1 John 4:17), so His righteousness still smells sweet within you, even when your actions stink!

The book of Song of Solomon is a love poem between Solomon and his wife. It is also an allegory of Jesus' love for His beloved church. Isn't it fascinating that the "Song of Songs," as the Hebrews call it, is a picture of Jesus' love for you and me? The highest form of singing is Jesus telling us how much He loves us.

In Song of Solomon chapter 5, the bride tells a story of how she has bathed and settled into bed for the night when her lover comes knocking at the door. She is too tired to get up and open the door, and He passes by, unwelcome to enter the room in intimacy. He doesn't divorce her for this action, nor does His wording of her become harsh and full of fury. In fact, the first words He says while standing outside of the door of her heart are, "Open for me, my sister, my love, my dove, my perfect one" (verse 2). Did you notice that He called her perfect? Even though she is slumbering, He still calls her perfect. Beautiful!

I hope that you can now see why we made the statement early in this chapter about how dangerous the modern teaching of a Great Awakening can be. Now we know there is certainly a need for an awakening, but we also know that it will have nothing to do with our works or efforts and everything to do with His glorious finished work.

Believer, it is high time for us to awake from our sleep. We have been lulled away from relationship and into a religion of works and performance. Slowly but surely, many of us have fallen asleep to the great truth of the righteousness of God in us through Jesus Christ. Sins and addictions are resurfacing in many lives, because we are always focusing on our abilities and unfinished works rather than resting in His beautiful finished work. You are still His beloved, and in His eyes, you are still undefiled. As we move on through this great adventure together, I yell it again, "Wake up!"

Good chapter

Falling into Grace | 5

Run, John, run, the law commands,
But gives us neither feet nor hands.
Far better news the gospel brings:
It bids us fly and gives us wings.
—John Bunyan, "Pilgrim's Progress"

We have said a lot about our sins being judged in the body of Christ and of His wonderful exchange, giving us His righteousness. We have also made several mentions regarding God's grace and how the New Covenant provides us with all things based on His finished work and no works of our own. Earlier, we promised we would explore that wonderful grace in more detail, and I am sure there is no better time than right now to do just that. A better understanding of God's grace will help further us along to the place we all desire to be.

I have heard an acronym made of the word "grace," and though I don't know who originated it, I think it is fitting: *G*od's *R*iches *A*t *C*hrist's *E*xpense. That little statement properly sums up what grace is all about. God, who is rich in all things, greatly desires to put that wholeness, health, goodness, and righteousness into mankind. Due to Christ's sacrifice at the cross, He can filter to us everything that He has in store. Paul said that God has forgiven us, "for Christ's sake" (Ephesians 4:32). Actually, all that God does to us and for us is for Christ's sake, as it is Christ who has paid it all.

An important starting point in the understanding of God's grace is to realize that grace is not a thing, a doctrine, a philosophy, or an idea. Grace is a *person,* and His name is Jesus! John's Gospel put it this way:

43

"For the law was given by Moses, but grace and truth came by Jesus Christ" (John 1:17 KJV).

When God's law arrived, it was *given* to us by the man Moses, but when God's grace arrived, it *came* to us by the man Jesus Christ. Notice that one was "given," while the other "came." This denotes that Jesus was not the carrier of grace in the same manner in which Moses was the carrier of the law but, rather, that grace and truth actually exist as more than objects and were embodied in Jesus. Jesus Himself put it this way, "'I am the way, the truth and the life'" (John 14:6). He doesn't say that He gives the truth but that He *is* the truth.

Paul's letter to Titus shows us that he also viewed grace as more than an idea when he says, "For the grace of God that brings salvation has appeared to all men, teaching us that, denying ungodliness and worldly lusts, we should live soberly, righteously, and godly in the present age" (Titus 2:11, 12). Paul says that grace has "appeared" and that grace teaches us how to live right. The arrival of God's grace toward man is thus embodied in someone who can "appear." Again, that someone is Jesus.

In light of these facts, it is necessary to see the message of the New Covenant as one composed entirely of grace, since Christ is both the originator of the covenant and the bringer of grace. The message of Christianity thus becomes a "message of grace." Where grace is removed from the message, Jesus is removed; when Jesus as grace is diluted or removed, Christianity becomes a religion of works and effort, right alongside every other belief on the planet.

Why should we remove the beauty of Christianity so that it is cheapened to be like all other beliefs? Every religion has its prophet, its book, and its ultimate destination, but only Christianity has grace! Grace is the undeserved favors of God, and no other faith's deity provides all things as a gift, through no works on the part of the recipient. We are truly blessed!

Not only is it necessary to see the New Covenant as a message of grace, it is essential that we make up our mind about how we feel about the ministry of the Apostle Paul. You will notice that I refer to this great apostle quite a lot and will do so even more as this book continues. The reason for this is that Paul was the first person to write down the concepts and ideas of the New Covenant, linking Christ's death on the cross to the prophecies of the Old Testament. An educated Jew, Paul divorced salvation from works and law and linked it to faith and grace. He paid for this

44

message with his life, but it was a life devoted not only to the preaching of grace but to the preaching of grace in a most radical way. He said this of his ministry:

"But I make known to you, brethren, that the gospel which was preached by me is not according to man. For I neither received it from man, nor was I taught it, but it came through the revelation of Jesus Christ" (Galatians 1:11, 12).

The reason that it is essential to settle in your heart how you feel about Paul's ministry is because his ministry was one composed entirely of grace. He called his message, "the dispensation of the grace of God," and felt that it was given to him to give to all of us (Ephesians 3:2). You won't find the fullness of his message in the Old Testament in either the law or the prophets, for as he said it, "was not made known to the sons of men, as it has now been revealed by the Spirit to His holy apostles and prophets" (Ephesians 3:5).

His message was so radical that he was often misinterpreted and had words put in his mouth, so to speak. Any examination of the message of grace will ultimately lead to the revelation Paul had and will actually end with the apostle as well, as he said, "If anyone preaches any other gospel to you than what you have received, let him be accursed" (Galatians 1:9).

As we have seen, when the Apostle Paul received the revelation of the New Covenant, he called it "the gospel." Most of us are aware that the word "gospel" means "good news," but have you ever considered that much of what we are hearing as gospel doesn't sound much like good news at all? Why is this?

Friend, grace is good news! Jesus paid for all of our sins and sicknesses in His body on the cross so that we might live the abundant life. The good news is that God is not angry with us, nor will He condemn us. The good news is that we are accepted in the beloved Son of God and that we have been declared His righteousness. The good news is that we are not judged on merit or worthiness, but our judgment is based on what we have done in our hearts with Jesus. Anything less than these things should be considered bad news and is never on par with "the gospel."

Paul said it this way:

"For I am not ashamed of the gospel of Christ, for it is the power of God to salvation for everyone who believes, for the Jew first and also for the Greek" (Romans 1:16).

The Apostle felt that there was no cause to be ashamed to preach the wonderful good news of God's grace through Jesus Christ, for only the preaching of grace can bring salvation to everyone who will accept by faith.

Now that we are digging deeper into God's grace and seeing Jesus and grace as one in the same, I want to make it clear that grace is not a New Testament concept exclusively. Grace was not an afterthought by God, saved until the arrival of Jesus. Grace has always been available to man throughout God's word. The first mention of grace is found in Genesis 6:8: "But Noah found grace in the eyes of the LORD." In the Old Testament, man had to find grace: in the New Testament, grace finds man! This is made possible, because man is now accepted in the eyes of God through the sacrifice of Jesus, thus the man who receives Jesus is automatically receiving God's grace.

We will deal with the law and how to identify it in more detail in a later chapter, but for now, I want to shine the light brightly upon grace. Recognizing God's grace will bring greater freedom and a renewed passion for the things of God.

The following "equations" might help us to understand better this important topic:

LAW = WORKS
GRACE = FINISHED WORK

Great Point!

Thus,

LAW = RELIGION
GRACE = RELATIONSHIP

When you function under a system of laws, you are bound by your works and judged by your work. When you function under the system of God's grace, you are held together by His finished work at Calvary. This gives us "religion" or "relationship." In religion, you are trying to live in a way that will please a God who is hard to please. If you do a good enough job, you are rewarded and will ultimately end up in heaven (or some other name, depending on your religion). In relationship, someone has gone to great lengths to pay for the things you can't pay for, and you are accepting it based on the free gift of grace. Though you do not deserve this gift, it is yours based on no works you have done: you simply accept it by faith.

Simply put, this is why Paul said, "For by grace you have been saved through faith, and that not of yourselves; it is the gift of God" (Ephesians 2:8).

The law brings religion, because it stands in the way of relationship. With a list of things holding you back from righteousness, it is impossible to truly know God personally. This is why God refused to show His face to Moses on request, going so far as to say, "no man shall see Me, and live" (Exodus 33:20). God's compromise was to cover Moses' face with His hand and then walk past him, removing His hand as He went so that Moses could see God's back (Exodus 33:23). The best that law can offer is a look at God walking away.] Good !

Then came Jesus, and as you have learned, then came grace! As He journeyed to the house of Jairus to heal his daughter, a woman with a bleeding condition elbowed her way through the crowd and grabbed hold of the hem of Jesus' garment as He passed by. She grabbed in faith, believing that Jesus could heal her disease, and immediately she received what she came for. Jesus stopped, felt power leave His body, and then an amazing thing occurred:

"And He looked around to see her who had done this thing" (Mark 5:32).

Under law, God refused to allow Moses to look at His face, but in this story, under grace, Jesus intentionally looks this woman in the eye. Where religion keeps even the best of us at a distance from God, relationship takes the worst of us and makes us part of the family. Jesus calls her "Daughter" (Mark 5:34), establishing a family relation with her that no religion and law could ever allow. Hallelujah for the arrival of grace!

Saint, please see yourself as a son or daughter of God. When you function in relationship, you begin to identify with God as your Father and not your Master. Though He never ceases to be Master of all things, the New Covenant has provided us with the ability to call Him by a new name: Abba. This word means "Daddy" and it brings God to us in a way that no Old Testament saint ever had.

Jesus said that He had manifested His Father's name to His disciples (John 17:6). The only name of God that He gave in the gospels that had never been used before in the Old Testament was Abba, and Paul gave us permission to use it as well, when he said, "For you did not receive the spirit of bondage again to fear, but you received the Spirit of adoption by whom we cry out, 'Abba, Father'" (Romans 8:15).

Anything less than a relationship between you and God can lead to a frustrating, guilt-ridden way of life. In fact, the enemy functions at his best in the realm of guilt and condemnation, because all of his work revolves around making you think that God is angry or unpleased with you. This causes us to feel unforgiven and unaccepted—all because we did something wrong. When we do this, we are judging ourselves based on our actions and not on His finished work. Do you see how easy it is to go from trusting Him to trusting us?

I recently sat in a hospital waiting room with an elderly sister from our church. As we waited for the doctor's report, I asked her about her initial conversion experience. I love to hear how the older saints of the faith first came to know Christ and what they have learned in their many years of living for Him.

This sister testified of how she came to Christ as a teenager, when someone invited her to a revival service. She was so happy to know Him as her Savior and was overjoyed to know that He lived in her heart. One day as she was walking home along her dirt road, she slipped into a rut that had been formed by tires driving through mud, and she instinctively cursed aloud. She instantly heard a voice in her head, telling her that she was going to hell because she had said that word. She said that from that moment on, she felt so guilty that she literally felt unworthy to even go to church. For the next four decades, she drifted away from God, convinced that she was lost.

This seems extreme, doesn't it? How could one bad word make someone believe that she is going to hell? That's what I thought as I heard the story, but I soon began to realize that, although it seems extreme, it is also very real! Satan is so quick to point out our errors and to heap guilt and condemnation upon us that no matter what we have done, he can make us believe that our sin is too big and that we are not worthy of heaven.

"Pastor, how do you know that it wasn't the Holy Spirit in her heart convicting her of her sin? Perhaps she was just too immature in the Lord to know the difference."

A few chapters from now, we deal with the role of the Holy Spirit in the life of the believer, but for now, let me point out that "There is therefore now no condemnation to them which are in Christ Jesus" (Romans 8:1). Remember what we have already learned: Jesus bore your condemnation in His body on the cross so that you would not be condemned.

The author of Hebrews assured us that under the New Covenant of grace, "Their sins and their lawless deeds will I remember no more" (Hebrews 10:17), and the Apostle Paul quoted David, saying, "Blessed is the man to whom the Lord shall not impute sin" (Romans 4:8). The word "blessed" means "happy," so how happy could this sister be if the Lord is counting all of her sins against her after she has accepted Christ?

I have heard the argument that new Christians often can't tell the difference between conviction and condemnation and that when they are being dealt with by the Spirit, they can mistake it as the devil. If that be the case, the Holy Spirit and the devil are functioning on the same level, using guilt as a means of eliciting a response. This is confusion, of which Paul said that God never authors in our lives (1 Corinthians 14:33). Dear believer never forget your heavenly Father never uses guilt and condemnation on you. Instead, He leads and guides with righteousness, peace, and joy in the Holy Spirit (Romans 14:17), allowing the Holy Spirit in you to teach you all things (1 John 2:27).

The voice of condemnation and guilt that pounds at you is an attack of the enemy to cause you to fight your problems through your works and your effort. This is the opposite of what Jesus came to accomplish in your life. Under the law there is only a list of demands, providing no support in living up to those demands. Under grace, there are no demands beyond faith, with grace supplying *all* support in living righteous and holy.

"Surely you would agree that if we do certain things, we fall out of favor with God. Didn't the Apostle Paul even mention that we can 'fall from grace'?"

I do not agree that our actions make us fall either into or out of favor with God. For the record, "favor" and "grace" are synonymous terms in the Greek, so when you see one, you can readily insert the other. God's abundant grace comes to us by means of the finished work of Christ on the cross, thus all of God's favor is on us due to Jesus living in us. If my actions could cause God's favor to move out of my life, God's grace is in me and on me, whether or not I have earned it. That system has nothing to do with God's grace as it mirrors His dealings with man under the Old Covenant rather than the New.

To address the issue of falling from grace, let's go to the passage in question and get insight into how Paul viewed God's grace. We find it in his letter to the church at Galatia. The portion about falling from grace is at the end of the verse, but look at the whole verse, and notice what Paul says will cause someone to actually fall from God's grace:

"Christ is become of no effect unto you, whosoever of you are justified by the law; ye are fallen from grace" (Galatians 5:4 KJV).

Did you catch it? Nowhere in that verse does Paul even hint that when a believer sins he or she will fall out of God's grace. Instead, Paul states that when you seek to be justified by the keeping of the law, you render Christ completely ineffective in your life, thus you fall from God's grace. In other words, when you try to be righteous based on your works or your abilities, you are saying, "I don't need God's grace. Grace is a gift, and I don't want a gift; I want a salary!"

I realize that we may not phrase it quite like I did in that last paragraph, but, in essence, it is what we are saying. Paul said it this way: "Now to him that worketh is the reward not reckoned of grace, but of debt. But to him that worketh not, but believeth on Him that justifieth the ungodly, his faith is counted for righteousness" (Romans 4:4, 5). See how when you work for your goodness and your blessings it is God who owes you? On the opposite end of the spectrum, you simply believe in what Christ has done for you, and God counts that in your favor, seeing you as righteous. Which one do you want?

The fact that we can even fall from grace means that grace is on a higher level than the works we have fallen into. This means in God's eyes, His grace is much higher than any and all of our works. This is why Paul said, "For sin shall not have dominion over you, for you are not under law but under grace" (Romans 6:14). Since we are under grace, we are promised that sin will never dominate us, and that God's grace functions as an umbrella over our spirit man.

Paul was so radical about the power of grace that he said it this way: "But where sin abounded, grace abounded much more" (Romans 5:20). Here, Paul firmly states that no matter how great the sin level is in someone's life or in the world around us, there is an abundance of grace available. The Greek word for "much more abound" has *huper* at the front of "abound," from which we get the English prefix "hyper" or "super." In other words, where there is sin, God has superabundant grace!

Paul preached this with such fervor that people began to accuse him of encouraging Christians to sin so that grace could be made to flow in their lives. He defended himself against these accusations by asking pointed questions like "Can we go on sinning so that grace may abound? God forbid! How can someone who is dead to who he used to be keep on living like he used to live?" (my paraphrase of Romans 6:1, 2). Do you see how Paul's message was so overwhelming that it scared the religious crowd of his day? Not much has changed in the response, but unfortunately, not many preachers are giving that crowd much to shout about regarding grace preaching either.

It is for this reason that I believe we should change our terminology regarding God's grace. Instead of saying that someone who sins has "fallen from grace," perhaps we should say that someone who sins has "fallen into grace." Since God's grace is waiting in abundance for every time we fall, may we encourage those around us not to fall? Instead, may we encourage those who have already fallen that grace is superabundant? Dare we be that radical?

"Pastor, you are taking this grace thing a bit too far. Perhaps you need to come back to the middle of the road, so to speak, concerning God's grace."

I use this statement, because I have heard that said about grace preaching. Some hear grace mentioned a lot, and they become afraid it will give people a license to sin. Let's use common sense: people sin whether you license their actions or not. Rather than fight over whether people feel "free" to sin, why are we not fighting to set men free? With millions upon millions bound within the confines of religion and works, too many are shying away from the same message that the Apostle Paul claimed would bring liberty and freedom, given to him straight from the lips of Jesus.

When the argument is made that we should "return to center," there is an unspoken belief that the preaching of grace should always be counterbalanced by the preaching of God's law. Jesus warned us of this in the Gospels:

> "No one puts a piece from a new garment on an old one; otherwise the new makes a tear, and also the piece that was taken out of the new does not match the old. And no one puts new wine into old wineskins; or else the new wine will burst the wineskins and will be spilled, and the wineskins will be ruined. But new wine must be put into new wineskins, and both are preserved" (Luke 5:36–38).

Jesus makes it clear that you cannot mix that which is new (New Covenant) with that which is old (Old Covenant). Any mixture is going to bring ruin and disaster, for the new way cannot agree with the old. To ensure that both the wine and the bottles are preserved, they must be the same. Notice that Jesus doesn't mention the possibility of putting old wine into old bottles for what He speaks of is always new.

Watch the follow-up verse and see if you recognize why we are slow to accept the New Covenant and quick to embrace the old:

Sermon
That
Change!

"And no one, having drunk old wine, immediately desires new; for he says, 'The old is better'" (Luke 5:39).

Our natural tendency is to resort back to the Old Covenant manner of getting what we deserve rather than the New Covenant way of God's grace and favor. Arguments about "balancing" our grace are uninformed, Old Covenant arguments. According to these statements of Jesus, what man calls "balance," God calls "mixture." This mixture cannot work, for the New Covenant is so much greater in scope and in power that it will shatter the stability of the Old Covenant if we try to make these two coexist.

"Should we just throw out our Old Testament?"

Absolutely not! Just place each covenant in its proper place. Know that everything in the Bible is inspired by God and written for our instruction, but not everything in the Bible is written to us. Do you see the difference? Though written *for* us, it is not all *to* us, because some things are pointed to a very specific audience. We will deal with this in more detail later, as we investigate the dividing line of the Bible. For now, I want to point out one specific and marvelous usage of the "old bottles."

Remember, we don't house the New Covenant message of grace within the framework of Old Covenant laws. If we try, grace spills out as useless, and the Old Covenant shatters in its rigidity. Instead, we use the Old Testament as a book of shadows to show us the substance that is provided in the New Testament. Let's watch and learn as Jesus does this for us first.

On the day of His resurrection, Jesus appears to two of his disciples on the road to Emmaus. This seven-mile journey from Jerusalem becomes one of utmost importance not only to them but to all of us, as Jesus blinds their eyes from knowing who He is so that He can reveal Himself in a most marvelous way. Rather than show His hands and His feet, which would convince them that He is Jesus, He does this:

And beginning at Moses and all the Prophets, He expounded to them in all the Scriptures the things concerning Himself" (Luke 24:27).

Jesus used the Old Testament to bring substance to the shadows, giving them a personal revelation as to who He was. This is awesome, because Jesus was using Scriptures that are still in our Old Testament. If He pointed them out, we can point them out. Better yet, if they saw Jesus through the Scriptures, we, too, can see Jesus through the Scriptures. Hallelujah!

Where we often make our mistake is when we take the Old Testament and preach it as if the cross never happened. When we treat the Old Covenant this way, we are doing damage to the finished work of Christ by placing the burden of living the Old Covenant on the backs of people. Jesus came to fulfill all of the demands of that law, and praise God, He did it.

I am unashamed to say that I am now radical about God's grace. I have become convinced that this message truly is the power of God unto salvation, and it doesn't end there. Where many pulpits preach God's grace as the answer for sinners, they then preach law and works for the believers. Paul disagreed, and so do I! Look at the next verse after the infamous "not ashamed of the gospel" statement:

"For in it the righteousness of God is revealed from faith to faith; as it is written, 'The just shall live by faith'" (Romans 1:17).

Only within the preaching of the grace of God is the righteousness of God revealed. When someone places faith in Christ, he is born again. After this, he does not reveal God's righteousness by a rigid set of moral instructions and laws, rather, he shines forth His righteousness "from faith to faith." In other words, the same faith and grace that saved you is the same faith and grace that will lead you to live the way a Christian should live. *Good!*

Being a radical about the grace of God is necessary in this hour, where only the radical voice can be heard. Throughout history, change has been affected by men and women who continue to shout about and talk about what others view as no big deal. It is often necessary for someone to "go overboard" in order for the rest of the world to pay attention. I believe this is why Paul presented grace so radically in his epistles. It was necessary to be radical about grace in a church culture so enamored with works and law.

I hope that now you can see that we are what we are only by God's grace. All of our goodness and blessing, our health and wholeness, our joy and peace are because of the wonderful, marvelous grace of God. We have all of these things because of our Christ within us. He is not only our Savior, our Lord, and our Friend, He is truly our grace!

Paul said of himself, "By the grace of God I am what I am" (1 Corinthians 15:10). You, too, can rest assured that whatever you will become, you will be that way because of the grace of God. One of the reasons that you may be reading this book is because you have an issue in your life that you desperately want rid of, or perhaps you feel bound by religion and weary of works, and someone put this in your hands to give you freedom and hope. Either way, when it is all said and done, we can all proclaim that it is only by God's grace that we become what we become. Since Jesus paid for everything at Calvary, all of our transformation is in the hands of God's grace, and due to those nail scars, they are very capable hands!

Has this chapter seemed a bit radical? If so, I respond, "Good! Mission accomplished!" It is going to take a return to Pauline principles regarding redemption and sanctification to become the people we all are so desperate to be. That return has been longed for and desired by many generations, and I am so excited to be a part of it now.

˷ My friend, I believe that if something is to be done to change our direction, it must be done quickly and radically. People are depending on it and on us. Are you ready?

The Scripture that Changed My Life | 6

If you are like me, you take a moment and scan the table of contents in a book to see what the chapters are titled. If that is the case, this chapter probably stood out in your mind as one that you would be extra interested in reading. I mean, if you went so far as to pick up a book about transforming your life, you must have a reason for doing so, and a chapter in that book about one verse that helped turn around the author would be extremely appealing. That might have prompted you to flip ahead to this point in the book to read this chapter first, or to at least read enough to find out what Scripture it was that changed my life. If I have just described you, stop! Please read the first five chapters before proceeding. Principles covered in those chapters are important in relation to this one, so I highly recommend reading them.

We know that faith comes by hearing, and hearing comes by the Word of God (Romans 10:17), so, in order for our faith to increase in a certain area, it is necessary to hear Scripture concerning that area. I have used the first five chapters of this book to unveil the beauty of the New Covenant so that your faith will grow and to prepare you for the fresh bread of this chapter. There was a solid basis of faith in my heart concerning the finished work of Christ when I arrived at the point in time where a revelation of grace became a necessity in me. I hope that faith is growing in you also. With that said, I realize that if I was actually describing you in the opening paragraph, you are obviously still reading, in spite of my warning.

My title for this chapter is perhaps a bit misleading. I don't believe that any one Scripture can truly change your life. As I previously explained, it took more than one to change mine. If simply reading a Scripture could transform us, Jesus would not have had to die; He could have simply spoken, and the Scriptures would provide life. But the words of Jesus cannot take a man from darkness to light, from sin to salvation, or from bondage to freedom. It took the entire finished work of Christ on the cross to bring permanent change to the hearts and lives of mankind.

I do, however, believe that God can pour the light of revelation into a verse in a timely moment in our lives, making an impact on us in a way it may never have before. When this happens, we begin to see the entire Bible differently, as the collective whole of Scripture is washed over in the same light as the singular verse. Life experiences that brought us to that place in the days, weeks, or even years preceding that particular verse coming to life in our heart, have actually prepared us for that revelation. Our Father knows what we need to hear, and He knows how to get us to the place to accept that which we hear, as if we are hearing or seeing it for the very first time.

For me, that verse was nestled into the Apostle Paul's instructions to the church at Corinth. Though I had read this particular passage countless times before, I will never forget the moment I questioned it in a way that I had never considered. In light of the context of the verse and the circumstances surrounding its usage, I was forced to look deeper into the Word to find what the apostle meant when he said it and why he felt he should even say it at all.

> "All things are lawful for me, but all things are not helpful. All things are lawful for me, but I will not be brought under the power of any." (1 Corinthians 6:12)

I hope that you can feel the power that is packed into the statement, "All things are lawful for me." It is important to remember that these words are being written to us by a man who knew the Law of Moses so well that he called himself a Pharisee (Philippians 3:5), which is a reference to a sect within Judaism that upholds the keeping of the law as the means of beholding God's righteousness (Philippians 3:6). After placing faith in Christ, Paul no longer felt that law-keeping could bring us that righteousness, for he wrote that if righteousness could come by the law, "then Christ died in vain" (Galatians 2:21).

For Paul to have come to a place where he would deny righteousness by the keeping of the law is one thing, but for him to go so far as to say that *all* things are lawful to him is quite another. This is a revolutionary concept for a man so in tune with the Mosaic Law. He is stating that not only is he not bound by the law for his righteousness, he is not bound to the law at all!

As the light of revelation is being turned on regarding this verse, let's take a deeper look within the text to find out what prompted the Apostle Paul to make such a radical statement. We will find myriad problems faced by the Corinthian church, many of which still stalk the church. We may also be introduced to a whole new way of preaching and teaching, one shaped by who we are in Christ rather than by how we are acting in our flesh.

In an earlier chapter, we briefly discussed how Paul dealt with sin in the church at Corinth. We commented that many sinful practices were happening among the people. Let's get a bit more specific at some of the things that Paul had to face in dealing with these young believers.

- Division and contention among the people about who is superior based on who led them to Christ (1 Corinthians 1:11–13)

- Carnal Christianity; spiritual milk drinkers rather than meat-eaters; "babes in Christ" (1 Corinthians 3:1–3)

- Incest between a church member and his stepmother (1 Corinthians 5:1)

- Christians suing Christians in secular court (6:1–8)

- Christians sleeping with harlots (6:15–18)

- Arguments concerning what was lawful to eat and drink (1 Corinthians 8 and 10:23–33)

- Christians getting drunk on communion wine (1 Corinthians 11:21)

- Instructions on how, when, and why spiritual gifts should be used, instead of the free-for-all attitude with which the Corinthian believers were using them (14:1–40)

This list makes it obvious that the Corinthian church had some real problems! Paul had a lot of work to do to bring them into a place of right-living, and how he goes about it is the key to what he thought of the grace message.

First and foremost, I want you to notice what Paul does *not* do. He doesn't threaten the believers with backsliding and hell, and he doesn't call them names. There is no mention of a curse falling upon the church, and he says nothing of them being distanced from the Holy Spirit. In fact, notice that Paul uses what I call the habit of reinforcement to bring believers to their senses.

The habit of reinforcement is how Paul preaches and teaches to convince the Corinthian church who they are in Christ. It requires Paul to affirm and reaffirm foundational truths about who they are in Christ due to Him entering their heart. This habit shows up frequently throughout his letters as a sign that he felt believers who fail need the truth about who they are in Christ drilled into them over and over again. Within that same list of problems and sins within the Corinthian church, Paul reinforces the believer's right-standing in Christ while refraining from attacks and threats.

In order to help our understanding of Paul's method of ministry, we will confine our study to the verses surrounding our key text. On one side of, "all things are lawful," we have Christians suing Christians in secular court, and on the other side, we have Christians sleeping with harlots. Due to the placement of these admonishments, let's consider the "sandwich" that Paul has constructed. The two pieces of bread are sins, with the meat being our key verse.

Right out of the gate, when dealing with the Christians going to court, Paul poses a question that harkens back to things that these believers should already know: "Do you not know that the saints will judge the world? And if the world will be judged by you, are you unworthy to judge the smallest matters? Do you not know that we shall judge angels? How much more, things that pertain to this life?" (6:2–3).

Do you see what Paul just did? His habit of reinforcement was to ask them, "Don't you already know these things?" This is reinforcing what they should already know and who they are, Paul thinks that because someday the church will judge angels, we should be able to judge ourselves now, without the input of the world. To go before them with matters pertaining to the church is to lower ourselves from a position of excellence to one of dependence.

Believer, some things in life should be viewed as simply beneath your station. There is no threat of hell in this text, aimed at saints to "scare them straight." However, there is an appeal to the believers to remember who they are and to get back to living up to the high place into which they are called. As a child of God, you have inheritance in Christ; slopping hogs should be considered way beneath you.

If you have been president of the United States, you don't run for mayor of your hometown. It would seem beneath "Mr. President" to suddenly become "Mr. Mayor." Is it wrong? Of course not, but it should feel that way to the president, and anything less than that which fits a child of God should feel the same way to you and me.

"Pastor, what about verses 9–10, where Paul warns us that certain people will not inherit the kingdom of God? Isn't this a threat of hell toward those who won't stop doing wrong?"

I have heard 1 Corinthians 6:9–10 used to scare the church about the possibility of a believer suffering in hell. Let's look at what Paul says exactly.

> "Do you not know that the unrighteous will not inherit the kingdom of God? Do not be deceived. Neither fornicators, or idolaters, nor adulterers, nor homosexuals, nor sodomites, nor thieves, nor covetous, nor drunkards, nor revilers, nor extortioners will inherit the kingdom of God" (1 Corinthians 6:9, 10).

Paul starts with a question and then ends with the answer. The sum of the verses is that the kind of people listed therein will not go to heaven, thus they will end up in hell. It is important to note not only what Paul says but *where* Paul says it. As we pointed out, the preceding verses have been dealing with Christians suing other Christians in secular court: "and that before the unbelievers" (verse 6). The question of verse 9 is to show the believer exactly what kind of person they are submitting themselves to. Paul is asking, "Don't you realize that the very people that you are asking to settle your disputes are in no qualified position to do so? Look at who they are! They are not even going to heaven!"

Then, just to make sure that the Corinthian believers don't think he is accusing them of being these things, Paul adds this awesome verse:

> "And such were some of you. But you were washed, but you were sanctified, but you were justified in the name of the Lord Jesus and by the Spirit of our God" (1 Corinthians 6:11).

I think the first part should be shouted from the pulpits to the pews: "And such *were* some of you!" Notice the past tense usage of "were." Even though the believers at Corinth are obviously full of problems, Paul sees them as a bunch of people who used to be on their way to hell, but now they are washed, sanctified, and justified by the power of the Holy Spirit.

I love the fact that Paul was not afraid to reinforce who these believers were in spite of the fact that they were not necessarily living that way. He is so confident in the ability of the Holy Spirit to change their lives with no effort on their part that he is willing to draw their eyes away from their issues and onto the power of the Spirit that already dwells in them.

Saint, you are not who you used to be, even if you occasionally fall where you used to fall! A pig and a lamb can both fall into the same mud hole. The difference is that the pig will stay there and wallow around, while the lamb will jump out and look to get clean. You may have reveled in squalor before coming to Christ, but now you are washed!

Now, that covers the top piece of bread on our sandwich. Let's look to the other side of our key verse to see the bottom piece. In that section, Paul deals with fornication within the church, again appealing to previous knowledge.

> "Do you not know that your bodies are members of Christ? Shall I then take the members of Christ and make them members of a harlot? Certainly not!" (1 Corinthians 6:15).

And then again, just a few verses later.

> "Or do you not know that your body is the temple of the Holy Spirit who is in you, whom you have from God, and you are not your own?" (1 Corinthians 6:19).

Paul is not ignoring the fact that these believers have problems, but he also refuses to ignore the fact that these believers belong to Christ and that their bodies are the temple of the Holy Ghost. He does not say that their bodies were the temple of the Holy Ghost, but now that they have sinned, He is no longer there. There is no insinuation on Paul's part that they are any less sanctified now than they were before. Their standing in Christ is secure, even though their actions do not reflect Him.

I believe that due to the creative work of Christ within our hearts, we are not who we used to be before we came to Jesus. While our Christian experience changes us from one day to the next, our ultimate change happened when we were born again at salvation. Because we have the Holy Spirit living and dwelling in our hearts, any continuous sin on the part of a believer must be attributed to ignorance. Why else would Paul continuously ask the believers if they had forgotten what they already knew?

My first investigation into this text led me to ask some obvious questions. Why didn't Paul just invoke the awesome power of the law? He saw people committing fornication within the church, and he made no mention of the responsibilities of marriage under Mosaic Law. He knew that most of these believers knew the Ten Commandments forward and backward, yet he never quotes the mighty Seventh Commandment: "Thou shalt not commit adultery" (Exodus 20:14). Why would Paul fail to bring "hellfire and brimstone" down on these Christians?

The answer to these questions is the heartbeat of the New Covenant. Paul knew that reinforcing the law to believers was the spark that ignited sin in their lives. He told them later, in this very letter, "The strength of sin is the law" (1 Corinthians 15:56), and to the church at Rome, he states, "The commandment came, sin revived and I died" (Romans 7:9). This is the reason that he says to Corinth what we covered in a previous chapter: "Awake to righteousness, and sin not" (1 Corinthians 15:34).

"Pastor, don't you think that believers just need more willpower? Their problem isn't ignorance; it's just plain laziness!"

I can only pose that question because that is the way I used to preach! The odd thing is while I was hammering away at "lazy Christians," I was struggling with various areas in my own life. All the while, I had a very limited understanding of how finished the finished work of Christ was. In retrospect, my chief problem was not effort; it was ignorance. Until I comprehended the love of Christ for me, in spite of all of my problems, I struggled beneath the weight of performance-based Christianity.

The Apostle Paul shared my sentiments when he spoke of his own struggles with sin. He said, "For I know that in me (that is, in my flesh) nothing good dwells; for to will is present with me, but how to perform what is good I do not find" (Romans 7:18). Notice that he claims to have the willpower, but the ability to overcome still alludes him. In other words, he isn't lazy; he's just ignorant! Good.

Of course, Paul found the answer to his problem, and it is the same answer for you and me. It wasn't more will-power, effort, or any other hidden thing. The answer for Paul to overcome the various areas of failure in his life was the knowledge of who Jesus is. He said, "O wretched man that I am! Who will deliver me from this body of death? I thank God through Jesus Christ our Lord!" (Romans 7:24, 25). He found his deliverance not in things but in the person of Jesus Christ.

Armed with the knowledge of Christ's finished work and confident that believers need constant reinforcement of who they are because of that finished work, Paul inserts his most profound statement of the New Covenant. "All things are lawful unto me" now stands in stark contrast to dependence on works and performance. If all things are lawful, the law holds no dominion over Paul. If all things are lawful, to invoke the thundering power of the Mosaic Law or the Ten Commandments is to preach backward, as if moving away from the cross.

It is impossible for Paul to remain true to the spirit of the New Covenant if he continues to link a believer's salvation to his own performance instead of to Jesus'. This is not taking sin lightly; it is simply a refusal to take the cross lightly.

"Aren't you afraid that telling people all things are lawful for them will lead them to do some terrible things?"

I'm not afraid to proclaim this message, because the Apostle Paul wasn't afraid, and I take my cue on how to preach New Covenant from the man who preached it first. With that in mind, it is important to remember that if we are going to take our preaching tips from Paul, we must be quick to emphasize what he emphasized with the same passion, power, and fervor he did. We cannot just proclaim all things as lawful without also being radical about the message of grace and the reinforcement of the believer's standing. Paul was radical in his "all things are lawful" statement, but no more radical than he was about Jesus.

One of the problems I have noticed with some ministries that proclaim the message of grace is that they place far more emphasis on what we can do with our liberty than on the source of our liberty. The message of grace is not about a doctrine or a philosophy but about a person: the Lord Jesus Christ. When Paul declares all things as lawful, he can do so with no fear, because he has spent so much time establishing a higher morality through Christ's finished work. To designate all things as lawful is simply to place more emphasis on Christ having fulfilled the law rather than on man's liberty to do anything he wants.

"Even though all things are lawful for us, shouldn't we set some boundaries in our Christian walk?"

Great question! And the answer is found in the remainder of Paul's statement about all things being lawful. Let's look at the complete verse again.

> "All things are lawful for me, but all things are not helpful. All things are lawful for me, but I will not be brought under the power of any" (1 Corinthians 6:12).

Paul places borders on his liberty with the use of the conjunction "but." Though all things are lawful, not all things are expedient. The word "expedient" is translated "profitable" in Greek, and it shows us that Paul knew that he was free to do whatever, but some of his actions would not profit his spirit-man. He wanted nothing in his life that would not edify and build him up, and though he was free from the law in his actions, he chose only those that brought profit to his walk with the Lord.

He furthered the border by stating that though all things are lawful, "I will not be brought under the power of any." This warning is meant to show the believer that even though all things are lawful for them to do, some things will go from innocent to enslaving. This was Paul's warning about addictions and dependencies. If the believer finds himself in something that owns him, he is voluntarily giving himself over to a *thing* instead of His Lord Jesus. Paul found this unacceptable in his own life.

Shouldn't this be unacceptable in our lives as well? Believers ask me about "things" all of the time. "Can I do this?" and "Can I do that?" They wonder if a certain activity is okay for them. My answer is, "All things are lawful for you, because Jesus fulfilled the demands of the law at Calvary. But be sure that what you do doesn't control you instead of you controlling it."

We want to answer only to the call of our Lord Jesus. When other things in our lives begin to tell us when to wake up, when to go to sleep, when to feel happy, and when to feel sad, we have become a slave to their beckoning call. I want to answer to Jesus, not to an addiction! Though my activity is lawful, if it is holding me instead of me holding it, I want nothing to do with it. I don't need a list of laws to tell me that; I have the Holy Spirit instead.

Finally, Paul establishes a third border on our Christian liberty, when he repeats his statement about all things being lawful in chapter 10, verse 23. In this instance, he goes on to say that though all things are lawful, "not all things edify." The full impact of this verse is found in the next one, "Let no man seek his own, but every man another's wealth" (1 Corinthians 10:24 KJV). It is unfortunate that the word "wealth" appears here in the King James Version, as it is italicized and added by the translators. Its presence in this verse has led people to misinterpret what the Apostle Paul is saying. Paul is telling us that our Christian responsibility is to seek the growth of our brother or sister in Christ, even above our own desires. In that context, the edification of the previous verse means that though all things are lawful for me, not all things will build up my brother.

Paul was very serious about how his liberty was perceived in the eyes of other believers. Look at a few of his statements about how our activities should be checked in relation to others and their walk with the Lord.

[handwritten margin note: Question]

"But beware lest somehow this liberty of yours become a stumbling block to those who are weak" (1 Corinthians 8:9).

[handwritten margin mark: circled 12] "But when you thus sin against the brethren, and wound their weak conscience, you sin against Christ" (1 Corinthians 8:12).

"It is good neither to eat meat nor drink wine nor do anything by which your brother stumbles or is offended or is made weak" (Romans 14:21).

"Let each of us please his neighbor for his good, leading to edification" (Romans 15:2).

I think it is obvious through these scriptures that Paul felt a natural border should exist in our Christian liberty that ends where other men will not be built up. If each believer places these limits in their own lives, they will find that a higher level of morality will ensue than they have ever known while struggling under the law.

James called what we are talking about, "the law of liberty" (James 2:12). It is a brand-new law, established at Calvary through the sacrificial death of Christ, whereby we are free from the old law of sin and death and are now allowing Christ to live through us in the Spirit of life in Christ Jesus (Romans 8:2). Don't expect a lower level of morality to come about by the knowledge of freedom from the law. In fact, Paul said, "But now we have been delivered from the law, having died to what we were held by, so that we should serve in the newness of the Spirit and not in the oldness of the letter" (Romans 7:6).

You need no deliverance from something unless it is binding and restrictive, which is exactly what happens to those on whom we place more law. Christ has redeemed us from the curse of the law, and now we are free to live, serving Him in a new way by the Holy Spirit instead of the old ways of laws and commandments.

We will deal even more with the law in future chapters, as we unveil more and more of exactly what Christ has accomplished for all of us. For now, let's conclude our discussion of law with one more statement on what Christ's finished work provides for us concerning morality. Some will argue that reinforcing to believers who they are in Christ and reminding them that they are free from the law will not bring a higher standard of living to them. We will prove that generality wrong as we go, but let's state this now, so it can begin to sink in: *under grace, you will live better on accident than you ever did on purpose, while trying to keep the law*. It's a fact, and only living it out can prove it right or wrong.

Keep this in mind: Jesus did not die so that you would never sin again. If He did, He failed! I know that is a bold statement, but think about it. If Christ's death at Calvary was to ensure that I would never mess up again, I should obviously never mess up again. The only obvious thing I see is that I have messed up again! If you are honest, I think you will admit as much about your own life. He didn't die to take away my ability to sin, but He did die to take care of the sin issue. Remember, He was the Lamb of God, which, "takes away the sin of the world" (John 1:29), not "the sins of the world." There are still sins in the world, but the issue of sin binding man has been dealt with, and the answer is found in Jesus.

Late in this book is an entire chapter that covers the topic of dealing with sin in our life. We will dig in later and discuss the ongoing issue with failure and what we can expect to happen in our lives now that we know Christ. But before we get into that, I think it is necessary to shine more light on this glorious grace.

By nature of discussing such controversial topics and scriptures, there are probably many questions forming in your mind about the mighty message of grace. I know that when 1 Corinthians 6:12 took root in my heart, it sparked a firestorm of internal debate and questions, all of which led me deeper into my search for the truth of Christ. The end result is a change in the way we live, pray, function, and act—and even in the way we read our Bibles. Some call it a revolution, while others say it is a rebellion. You are beginning to formulate your own theory about that even as you read, so let's go a bit deeper into that thought. I want to show you the real job of God's grace. Are you ready?

Grace: Revolution or Rebellion? | 7

Do you realize that as believers in Jesus Christ, we have been given a great gift? Aside from the assurance that we are righteous through Christ's finished work and the joy that comes in knowing this, we hold within our hearts something so awesome and powerful that all of the powers of darkness wage a constant war against our understanding of it. You and I have been given the gift of God's grace, which brings us, "everlasting consolation and good hope" (2 Thessalonians 2:16). — Read

The Greek word for "consolation" denotes "encouragement," meaning that God's grace provides us with a constant source of encouragement through the finished work of Jesus. "Hope" means "a constant expectation of good." Put the two together, and you find that one of the chief provisions of God's grace in the life of all believers is to always encourage us and give us a reason to expect good things.

Don't think it selfish or bad to expect good things from God. Jesus said, "If you then, being evil, know how to give good gifts to your children, how much more will your Father who is in heaven give good things to those who ask Him!" (Matthew 7:11). Due to the grace of God, we can always be encouraged that our Father *is* working all things out for our good (Romans 8:28).

The underlying theme in this book has been the love of God and the loveliness of Jesus. We have accented that theme by showing that God is no longer angry with man because of the finished work of His Son on the cross. We have also tried to unveil the loveliness of Jesus, showing Him the way the Song of Solomon said He is: "altogether lovely" (Song of Solomon 5:16).

Up to this point, my prayer is that we have succeeded in making His love and affection irresistible. When love becomes irresistible, it becomes easy to "fall" into that love. You cannot make yourself love someone you find unattractive, and making yourself love a God of vengeance, anger, and demands is equally impossible. However, now that you are seeing God as loving and His Son as increasingly lovely, falling into love with His irresistible love should be easier by the page.

As with any other great truth, the message of God's love and grace has been vehemently opposed by the enemy, who simply cannot afford to have believers walking in this powerful knowledge. His attack against the good news is as old as the good news itself, and it prompted the early apostles to constantly remind the believer of who they were in Christ. Paul took the gospel of grace a step further and gave us sound instruction as to what every believer should expect from his or her own life.

"For you, brethren, have been called to liberty; only do not use liberty as an opportunity for the flesh, but through love serve on another" (Galatians 5:13).

While all of us want to know what "call" God has for our lives, there is a universal call for every believer. We are "called to liberty," meaning that our Christian lives are meant to be lived in a state of liberty, not of bondage. Any bondage that is imposed on us by others or by our own self is to live beneath the call of God.

Due to what we learned in the previous chapter about unseen boundaries on our Christian liberty now that we are under grace, we should take another step forward in our understanding of what it means to be free in Jesus. Christian liberty stands as a representation of what God's grace provides. Understand your liberty, and you walk in it. Walk in it, and you fulfill God's call in your life. Sounds pretty important, right?

The truth is, understanding what is happening inside of you is very important. I know that when I was turned onto the message of God's grace, I began to have conflicting emotions. The side of me that had spent decades reading the word and believing that I had it "down" was beginning to see a whole new side of God. It was like getting saved all over again! I formed questions in my heart so fast that I could hardly find answers to all of them. Slowly but surely, the message of grace began to quench my doubts and fears, and my heart settled on the peace afforded by the finished work.

One of the things that surfaced in my journey was the idea that the message of God's love and grace, the very message that we have been presenting in this book, was absolutely revolutionary. So incredible were the revelations that God was opening up through His Word that it felt like a revolt against so many of the things I had known—and preached. That kind of revolution is as life changing as it is obvious.

As glorious and revolutionary as the message of grace is, let us always be on guard that it not take a side step from the road of revolution and onto the path of rebellion. Though the actual words "revolution" and "rebellion" do not appear in the New Covenant in relation to the message of grace, their spirits are there, and we would do well to know the difference.

Looking at a secular definition of these two terms first, we get a better understanding of with what we are dealing. *Webster's New World College Dictionary* defines "revolution" as, "A complete or radical change of any kind." Conversely, it defines "rebellion" as, "A defiance of, or opposition to, any kind of authority or control." Good definitions -

Using these definitions, it appears safe to call what is happening in our hearts concerning the message of God's grace as a revolution. We have had a complete and radical change in our hearts concerning the way God thinks about and deals with us. To view the cross as a truly finished work, with no works of our own being needed, is a "radical change" from the idea that Jesus just helps us with our old man; thus, the message of grace is a "radical" message.

Grace as a revolution means that we are in the midst of a revolt, but not one of violence or protest. We are also not revolting against the organized church or ministry. The revolution that grace provides is a revolt against using the law or obedience to achieve righteousness. It is a revolt against religion in favor of a relationship. Grace is God shining light on the New Covenant, and to live in the revolution of God's grace is to refuse to glorify that which is abolished (2 Corinthians 3:13). We are considered revolutionaries, because we see the Old Covenant as, "that which decayeth and waxeth old, ready to vanish away" (Hebrews 8:13 KJV).

To see grace as a rebellion would require, by definition, that we defy all rules and regulations simply because they exist. We would answer to no one and recognize no authority, for we would deem authority as "part of the problem." We would purposely run opposite of "religion," just because we can. Anything that others say they cannot do, we would do, just to show them that we could. The very spirit behind using this and calling it "grace" is not one of discovery, and it in no way shines glory on Jesus. This is rebellion in its basest form. In other words, this is not the message of grace!

Please note: There is a difference between chasing grace for what it gives and chasing it for who grace is. Remember, grace is not a doctrine or a philosophy. It is a person, and His name is Jesus (John 1:17). To "use" grace is to "use" Jesus. He must always be glorified and lifted, so any message that draws attention to us instead of Him cannot truly be the message of grace. Good!

It is Jesus, not a message, that makes us who we are. The reason that grace revolts against religion in favor of relationship is because relationship is a unique quality about which no other religion can boast. We are in no way on par with the other religions of the world, for we have what they cannot have. It is the fact that God became a man and bore the sins of the world, sacrificing Himself so that all who believe by faith could have the very Spirit of God live in them for eternity, that makes our walk so unique. Jesus, not moral codes or ceremony, makes us different. His life inside of us makes us joint heirs with Him before the Father. As sons, we belong to a family, not a religion, and no other faith on the planet can say that.

Paul knew that living in liberty was going to be a challenge, because so much of our very nature runs opposite to the idea of a finished work. He opens the fifth chapter of Galatians with, "Stand fast therefore in the liberty by which Christ has made us free, and do not be entangled again with a yoke of bondage." "Stand fast," means that it will be a challenge just to stay in the freedom of Christ. His warning against being "entangled again" denotes that the believer used to be entangled in something, and we should watch out against being in it again.

"There's the key, Pastor Paul. The Apostle Paul is warning the believer about being entangled in sin now that they have been saved."

I whole-heartedly disagree! Read the verses that come between our key text (5:14) and the one that opens this chapter. At no point do you hear Paul mention anything about believers sinning, but you do hear him talk a lot about believers returning to the work of circumcision and the law. We will deal with some of these verses in more detail in a moment, but know that the bondage that Paul is warning us about is the bondage of trusting works for our righteousness.

"If Paul is warning us about works placing us under bondage, why does he say, 'Again'? Before you get saved, you aren't under the bondage of works; you're free to do whatever!"

Actually, you're free "to do whatever" now that you are saved. However, we know that doing "whatever" might bring reproach to the name of Jesus, shame to us and our families, and lead to legal and social consequences we can never take away.

Some argue against preaching radical grace, because they fear this message gives people a "license to sin." My response is that you sinned like crazy before you came to Christ, and no one gave you a license! Let's not put more confidence in our ability to tell people how to live than we do in the power of God's grace to change them. Reader, be perfectly honest with yourself. You wouldn't be reading this book if you had figured out how to change yourself, right? We all need God's grace to teach us how to live, because we are doing a terrible job of it through our own works.

Concerning the rest of the question, Paul says "again" because, contrary to popular belief, even the sinner is living and functioning under the law in one way or the other. Due to our widespread teaching of the law, particularly in America, most every sinner is law-conscious in how they govern themselves. Don't believe me? Ask the average sinner on the street how to get to heaven, and he will invariably respond with some form of law or works. You will hear things like, "Treat others the way you want to be treated," "Don't steal or kill or commit adultery," "Give to charity," or, "Do your best to be a good person." All of these responses completely omit God's grace.

The law-consciousness that we have created causes people a world of guilt and condemnation. Granted, most unbelievers don't live under near as much of this as many believers, because the sinner doesn't have the guilt and condemnation reinforced in him on a weekly basis, like most churchgoers! Also, notice that the knowledge of "morality" has in no way helped people live better. In fact, few could disagree that the morality of America has actually decreased, even though there are more churches—and more preaching—than ever.

"Pastor, you've hit on the problem! We have more churches but not enough preaching on sin. The church should be more sin-conscious if we are going to see people start living right."

Frankly, I disagree, and apparently so did the author of the book of Hebrews.

"For the law, having a shadow of the good things to come, and not the very image of the things can never with these same sacrifices, which they offer continually year by year, make those who approach perfect. For then would they not have ceased to be offered? For the worshipers, once purified, would have had *no more consciousness of sins*" (Hebrews 10:1, 2).

Do you see what the author is insinuating? If the sacrifices of the Old Covenant had actually changed people, they wouldn't feel the need to keep coming back to offer more sacrifices. If these sacrifices had actually cleansed them of their sins, they wouldn't remain sin-conscious!

"But in those sacrifices there is a *reminder of sins* every year" (Hebrews 10:3).

Every time someone under the Old Covenant offered a lamb for his sins, he was reminded of his sin. The author deems sin-consciousness as a bad thing, for it calls to mind the sins that we have committed. The fact that there was sin-consciousness meant that the sacrifice had not worked, thus the author writes the next verse.

"For it is not possible that the blood of bulls and goats could take away sins" (Hebrews 10:4).

Since no animal could remove the sin on the heart of the offender, they lived under the constant strain of guilt and condemnation. The sin-consciousness was due to the fact that he had not been sanctified by the sacrifice, for the sacrifice itself was an imperfect animal.

Then came Jesus! Perfect in every way, He was the total fulfillment of the law (Matthew 5:17). When He died, His sacrifice was, "for sins forever" (Hebrews 10:12), and this offering has, "perfected forever them that are sanctified" (Hebrews 10:14 KJV). All of my sins are beneath His sacrificial blood, and I am perfect in the eyes of the Father. Acknowledgment of this keeps me from living under guilt and condemnation and helps me to fulfill my call to liberty in Jesus.

Can you see how making people conscious of their sins actually takes the focus off of the sacrifice? When people under the Old Covenant felt sin-consciousness, it was because their sacrifices couldn't take away their sins. Jesus was the perfect sacrifice to take away our sins, so why would we remain conscious of them, as if the cross never happened? Sin-consciousness does not prove that you are a wise and sensitive believer. It simply proves that you still feel like the sacrifice is insufficient.

Paul's warning of seducing spirits and doctrines of devils being preached in the last days included people who have "their conscience seared with a hot iron" (1Timothy 4:2). The phrase "seared with a hot iron" is from the Greek word *kausteriazo* from which we derive the English word "cauterize". Its definition is "who carry about with them the perpetual consciousness of sin." His warning is that last-day ministries will cause people to carry a constant consciousness of their sin, and he calls this a doctrine of the devil!

In some circles, we have been led to believe that the more ceremony is involved in our Christianity, the better we are. In fact, some go so far as to measure the quality of their Christianity by their involvement in religious activities. Just after warning the Galatian church to stand fast in their liberty, Paul warns them of leaning to their ceremony for their self-worth.

"Indeed I, Paul, say to you that if you become circumcised, Christ will profit you nothing" (Galatians 5:2).

We can be certain that Paul does not mean that if you are a circumcised male there is nothing that Christ can do for you. Instead, Paul is referencing the Jewish rite of circumcision, by which the Jews considered themselves superior to the heathen world, as their circumcision was the sign of the covenant. Paul is pointing them away from the ceremony of religion to a higher covenant.

"And I testify again to every man who becomes circumcised that he is a debtor to keep the whole law" (Galatians 5:3).

Once any amount of law is added to your Christianity, all of the law must be added. We do not get to pick and choose the aspects of the law that we are going to keep in order to be declared righteous. Some believers will shout about keeping the Ten Commandments but then ignore the dietary laws of the Old Testament, which do not allow the consumption of shrimp, lobster, or pork. The moment that we trust any religious ceremony for righteousness, we are a debtor to the entire law. Good!

Stand fast in your liberty when someone presents you with the things that you must do, "In order to be a better Christian." Better Christian? What is better than trusting in Christ and His finished work for my righteousness?

In chapter 4, we dealt with what it means to "fall from grace." The Scripture that mentions falling from grace comes next within the context of these Scriptures in Galatians 5. I won't go over all of that information again, but I do want to reinforce that Paul is speaking of those who seek to be justified by what they do instead of who Jesus is. To do this is to fall from the protection of grace.

This message of grace is such a pride-busting message! The spotlight is taken off of us and our efforts and is shone directly onto Jesus. We get no glory, while He gets all of the glory. We get no credit, while He takes all of the credit. This is a revolution, for where man has been prodded and held up and supported in the past, the message of grace holds up nothing but Jesus and His finished work. We are not rebelling against a system, but we are revolting against a dead idea, and serving a living Savior!

In the midst of such a river of God's grace, there are still those who use their liberty in ways unbecoming of a child of the King. Paul's next verse of instruction covers both those who are doing things for their righteousness and those who are doing nothing at all.

"For in Christ Jesus neither circumcision nor uncircumcision avails anything, but faith working through love" (Galatians 5:6).

We have established that trusting in a work, like circumcision, can offer you no hope, but Paul goes a step further and states that even those who trust in "uncircumcision" have no hope. In other words, you can't put any more trust in the fact that you don't do certain things than someone else can in the fact that they do them. Let me give you an example.

One believer feels that he must go to church every time the doors are open, or he will disappoint the Lord. No matter how he feels or what is going on in his life, he is at church, "come hell or high water." Another believer feels he doesn't have to be there every time in order to maintain his salvation. He knows that he is God's righteousness anyhow, so occasionally he does something else while his brother is at church. The first man could learn to boast about his church attendance, lording it over everyone around him that "We good Christians don't miss church." The second man could boast just as easily, though it is an unfamiliar boast to many of us not raised in the atmosphere of radical grace. His boasting might sound more like, "Boy, I feel sorry for those of you who think you get something more by going to church. You are so deceived. Someday, maybe you will grow up in the Lord and realize that your works don't work."

Neither brother is operating in much love, right? In fact, notice that Paul concludes verse 6 by stating that faith works by love. Our ability to walk in the liberty of God's grace is hampered whenever that walk isn't coupled with love. To the church at Corinth, Paul said something similar when he said, "Knowledge puffs up, but love edifies" (1 Corinthians 8:1).

Where the second brother in our example has obviously been impacted by a revelation of grace, he is dangerously close to letting a revolution turn him into an unsightly rebel! To use your grace to, "Show them I am as saved as they are," is to abuse the beauty of grace for self-gain. There is no room for showing up others when we are living in the love that grace provides. Don't stop reading the Word, or praying, or giving, or going to church just to show someone that you don't have to do those things in order to be righteous. Living in that manner is allowing someone else to dictate your actions based on the law. That is rebellion, and that is bondage!

I do all that I do because I love to see Jesus and living in His daily grace shows me His blessed face. Don't do things to get things, and don't avoid things to avoid getting things. Do things because you are His child. This will lead to a better life and better living, as you live like He would live, with no law telling you to do so.

Earlier in his letter to Galatia, Paul called the Galatian Christians "foolish" (Galatians 3:1). This marks the only time I can find that Paul ever calls a believer a fool. Notice that it doesn't come after some horrendous sin (he never called the obviously carnal Corinthians "foolish"), but in a statement about their thinking righteousness can come through their actions.

"O foolish Galatians! Who has bewitched you that you should not obey the truth, before whose eyes Jesus Christ was clearly portrayed among you as crucified? This only I want to learn from you: Did you receive the Spirit by the works of the law, or by the hearing of faith? Are you so foolish? Having begun in the Spirit, are you now being made perfect by the flesh?" (Galatians 3:1–3).

Remember that the author of Hebrews said Christ has perfected forever those who are sanctified (Hebrews 10:14). If Christ has done it, how much more perfect than perfect can you get? Can we be made "better Christians" by our actions? Paul didn't think so, and he thought it foolish to believe otherwise.

Now, with that text in mind, let's jump back into the context of chapter 5, where Paul says, "This persuasion does not come from Him who calls you. A little leaven leavens the whole lump" (Galatians 5:8, 9). Paul is reminding them that they must have picked up this knowledge of personal sanctification somewhere else, for he certainly didn't teach it to them. Also, just as a little yeast in the dough makes the whole bread rise, a little law in the living binds the whole of our liberty.

If the Galatian church didn't get these ideas about righteousness and sanctification from the Apostle Paul, they must have gotten them from false doctrine and the enemy. Where might we be getting our similar ideas? Paul was a preacher of radical grace, and a return to his gospel is a necessity if we are going to see believers living in their God-given liberty again today.

Let's go back to the place we started in this letter to the Galatians and sum up Paul's idea of a grace revolution.

> "For you, brethren, have been called to liberty; only do not use liberty as an opportunity for the flesh, but through love serve one another" (Galatians 5:13).

Remember two things about this passage:

1. Don't use your liberty as an occasion to get by with sin. Frankly put, you are better than that, and to live in such a manner is so far beneath you as to be considered embarrassing. If you are dwelling there, you have found that it is by no means easy to live in that manner since you are born again. Shake off the dust of condemnation, and move on from this point forward. This freedom is a revolution, not a rebellion.

2. Don't use your liberty as an occasion to show off your liberty. This is an act of drawing attention to yourself, which leaves no glory for Jesus. Paul was determined to have no part in this, going as far as to say that he would not glory, except in the finished work (Galatians 6:14).

The Apostle Peter preached a similar message, encouraging Christians to live in such a high manner that they would, "put to silence the ignorance of foolish men" (1 Peter 2:15). He then compliments Paul's ministry by telling all of us how to live.

> "As free, yet not using liberty as a cloak for vice, but as bondservants of God" (1 Peter 2:16).

"Maliciousness" is "wicked or evil," so Peter is telling us to be free in Christ, but not to use that freedom as an excuse to be wicked or to perform evil. Do you see how both of these early church leaders preached the liberty of grace as a revolution?

I am aware that people are possibly going to abuse the message of grace, and that is one of the reasons I am so passionate about preaching grace radically and right. Peter and Paul had to know that people would take the message of liberty and run with it, often taking it out of bounds. This knowledge didn't make them run back to the preaching of performance-based Christianity for fear believers couldn't handle the truth. Instead, it pressed them forward and deeper into a revolution that changed the world they inhabited. These revolutionaries were the ones who, "turned the world upside down" (Acts 17:6). How about we have a similar revolution and turn our world over in our generation?

If you have been with us from the beginning of the book, the foundation of grace has been properly laid. You have been faithful, and I pray you are now brimming with faith. The face of Christ is shining brighter and brighter, and we are going to unveil even more of His loveliness. As we approach the next chapter, the heartbeat of this book is about to thump loudly. For those who have been reading, looking for the change that you so desire, read on in faith. Your answer lies just around the corner.

Effortless Transformation | 8

I have injected several questions into the previous chapters to try and cover things that I think the reader may want to ask. This time, I want to start the chapter by asking a question of my own.

"Just how finished is the finished work?"

Jesus cried, "It is finished" (John 19:30), before He bowed His head and released His Spirit in death. We know what He meant by that phrase, as we have learned that the wrath of the Father was exhausted through judgment in the body of Jesus. Armed with the knowledge of what the finished work is, we should now establish just *how* finished that work is. What is finished, and what is not finished? What did He do versus what I am expected to do? Does "it is finished" deal with my redemption only or also with my transformation?

The fact that Jesus used this statement just before His death shows us that He is referring to all of the things that are required to pay the price for man's redemption. The finished work of Calvary was simply the physical fulfillment of something that was predetermined in the spirit. Revelation tells us that the Lamb (Jesus) was slain, "from the foundation of the world" (Revelation 13:8). And the author of Hebrews equates the finished work to the rest that a believer finds in Christ:

> "For we who have believed do enter that rest, as He has said: 'So I swore in My wrath, they shall not enter My rest,' although the works were finished from the foundation of the world" (Hebrews 4:3).

The work of Christ on the cross was a finished work in God's eyes from the time He created the heavens and the earth. Calvary was not an afterthought or a response to Satan's work. Calvary was the very reason that God created man in the first place. To express love toward humanity through the sacrifice of His own Son was God's original plan. Crucifying Christ and then raising Him from the dead was the total work of God, allowing the risen Christ to live through us.

Good. "For if when we were enemies we were reconciled to God through the death of His Son, much more, having being reconciled, we shall be saved by His life" (Romans 5:10).

I realize that we shared the previous verse with you in an earlier chapter, but now I hope you can see the finished work clearly as you read it. The death of Christ reconciled us to God, while the risen life of Christ provides salvation for us on a day-to-day basis. Thus, the finished work is so finished that even how we live our lives is effected by what Christ did at Calvary.

If I am saved by His resurrected life, which could only happen because of the finished work of the cross, my existence as a child of God is entirely dependent on the life of Christ within me. In other words, if it is finished, any transformation within me is his responsibility!

Jesus called Himself the vine and us His branches (John 15:5). He is the source of life, while we are simply an extension of that life. You can cut off a branch of the vine and do no damage to the vine, but if you cut the vine in half, all of the branches connected to that vine are destroyed. Jesus is saying that He is the source of life and hope and transformation, and we are merely the dressing on His vine. Our designation as branches gives us the right to view our experience as one of "being" and not only one of "doing."

We are called "human beings" and not "human doings" for a reason: God made us to be! Due to the fall of Adam in eating from the Tree of Knowledge of Good and Evil, our default position is one of works and effort. When we encounter a difficulty, we go to work to come up with a solution to solve the problem or to overcome the obstacle. Living in the finished work is seeing Christ as having paid in advance for the solution. Better yet, it is seeing that Jesus *is* the solution.

Jesus had an encounter with a man that epitomized the struggle of mankind to break free from the pattern of works for their righteousness. We refer to the man as the, "rich, young ruler," and in all three Gospel accounts of his conversation with Jesus, his approach is similar. Matthew records that he asks, "'Good Teacher, what good thing shall I do that I may have eternal life?'" (Matthew 19:16).

In this account, he asks what "good thing" he needs to do in order to have eternal life, but in Luke's Gospel, we find that he actually asks what he needs to do in order to "inherit eternal life" (Luke 18:18).

Inheritance is different than payment. A payment is something given in exchange for services rendered, while an inheritance is something that you receive because you are a family member and someone has left something for your provision. The ruler wants to know what good thing he can do in order to receive his inheritance. This young man is confused! You cannot "earn" an inheritance; you must be born into it. In other words, you don't receive an inheritance by what you do but by who you are. *Good,*

At some point in our Christian life, most of us have fallen into this familiar pattern of believing there is something we need to do in order to receive all that God has for us. I want you to notice that this young man is the only person in the Gospels who comes to Jesus asking for eternal life and leaves disappointed. When you approach God wondering what you can do for Him, the end result is heartbreak; however, when you approach Him based on what Jesus has done for you through the finished work, there is eternal life. *Good,*

Using the previous analogy of the vine and the branches, Jesus goes on to say that as branches, we are to produce good fruit. Now, let's take a closer look at that verse and see how the fruit is to come out of our lives.

"'I am the vine, you are the branches. He who abides in Me, and I in him, bears much fruit; for without Me you can do nothing'" (John 15:5).

There is no doubt that the fruit we produce will happen, because we are abiding in Him. But did you notice that Jesus reinforces the thought to close the verse? "Without me you can do nothing" is Jesus saying to us that the fruit will only grow as we are on the vine, for it is the vine that makes the fruit come out of the branch in the first place. *A Good*

Fruit production is effortless for the branch. The tree uses its roots to push down into the soil and bring nutrients to the branches. The tree reaches upward to the sun for its life-giving rays. It is the tree that holds the life and serves as the source, while the branch sees the fruit spring forth from its buds. The branch simply holds the fruit, while the tree does all of the work. Without the tree, the branch not only produces no fruit, it is actually wasting good space. *Good thought,*

If you own an orchard, you don't talk to your trees to get them to produce apples or oranges. You don't jump up and down on them or shake the branches at the right time of year in order to make the fruit spring forth. You realize that they will produce fruit when they are supposed to, and no amount of rushing or hurrying will make it come any faster.

Believer, you are a branch on the Great Vine, Jesus Christ. He is your source and your provision. His finished work paid for everything so that you can have the sweet fruit of the Spirit, springing forth from your life on a day-to-day basis. You will begin to produce His goodness effortlessly due to all of His efforts.

> **"Read on, Pastor. The next verse says that if you don't abide in Jesus, not only will you not produce fruit but you will be cast into the fire. This Scripture means that if you don't work for the Lord, you will cease to be a believer and end up in hell!"**

This verse should never be used to make a believer think that he might end up in hell if he doesn't work hard enough. It should actually be used to prove two important things, which are found in the details of the verse.

"'If a man abide not in me, he is cast forth as a branch, and is withered; and men gather them, and cast them into the fire, and they are burned'" (John 15:6 KJV).

Men have never had the power to send one another to hell. In this verse, it is men, not God, who are burning the branches. There is no mention of everlasting judgment or the flames of hell, but rather a bonfire, where nonproducing branches are burned up by the hands of men.

That fact leads us to the second and most important one. Your fruit production, or lack thereof, has a profound effect on what the world thinks of you and of Jesus. If you fail to abide near Jesus as your source, you will not produce the fruit of the Spirit. It is impossible for the Holy Spirit to work properly within your heart if you place no confidence in the finished work, for that is where He works! When you live in this manner, you make it easy for men to persecute and torment you, as there is nothing about your Christianity worth respecting. Good!

Inside every seed there is a code that dictates what that seed will become. If you put an apple seed in the ground, you will never grow an orange tree. It is impossible for the seed to become something other than what it is destined to become. You and I have a code inside of us that was placed there at our conversion. Christ has destined for us to produce fruit by the Holy Spirit, and as we rest in His finished work, the Spirit will do the job He was placed inside of us to do.

If we stress and wonder what "good thing" we can do to bring the fruit out in our lives, we will end up with "works" instead of "fruit." When Paul listed off the fruit of the Spirit in Galatians 5:22–23, he preceded it with a list called the "works of the flesh" (5:19–21). Until this point in Galatians, the book has been about the superiority of grace to law. When it comes time to reveal the work of the Spirit in the life of a believer, it remains necessary to show what happens if that believer interferes with fruit production. The end result is the works of the flesh, which come naturally to us in our effort to change ourselves.

"Pastor Paul, if my growth in Christ is compared to a tree producing fruit, what does it matter if I help? If the fruit is going to come out, isn't it going to come out even if I am working?"

Actually, it will *not* come out if you interfere, because our efforts can literally take what should have been simple and natural and make it impossible.

When my wife and I bought our first home, we were pleasantly surprised to find a little peach tree in the yard. I was excited at the possibility of that tree producing peaches every year, as I love a good, fresh peach. After the first year, I noticed that the tree produced peaches but not very many of them, and none were very large. I decided that the tree needed a little pruning, believing that removing a branch here or there would provide the others with more nutrients and help them to grow. Needless to say, not only did I not help the tree produce better peaches, I killed off the few it was producing in the first place! My lack of knowledge destroyed the fruit.

Now, someone might argue that if I had correct knowledge and knew just where and when to prune, I could have helped the tree produce better fruit, and he would be correct. The problem with applying that analogy to Christian growth is that Jesus anticipated our desire to play husbandman over the orchard.

"'I am the true vine, and my Father is the husbandman'" (John 15:1 KJV).

The only one with the rights to prune our spiritual tree is the husbandman, and that husbandman is the Father. When we prune through works and effort, we destroy what is already there. Only the husbandman knows when and where to prune. Let Him do the work!

God's Plan for Changing Man

God has a Master Plan for changing us. This makes sense, considering He is the One who made us. It is a process of several steps, all of which are encompassed and paid for within the finished work of the cross. Let's start with what we will call God's destiny for all of us.

"For whom He foreknew, He also predestined to be conformed to the image of His Son, that He might be the firstborn among many brethren" (Romans 8:29).

God's destiny for us is for us to be conformed into the image of Jesus. Before we get into what that means or how He plans on bringing that about, we must know that step one in God's process of changing us was to eliminate and eradicate completely the old man we were.

The death of our old man happened the moment we accepted Christ as our Savior. When we expressed faith in Christ, we were, "buried with Him through baptism into death" (Romans 6:4). Also, "Our old man was crucified with Him, that the body of sin might be done away with, that we should no longer be slaves to sin" (Romans 6:6). Because of this, you can, "Reckon yourselves to be dead indeed to sin, but alive to God in Jesus Christ our Lord" (Romans 6:11).

To the Corinthian church (yes, the same Corinthian church that had myriad moral problems), Paul said, "Therefore if anyone is in Christ, he is a new creation; old things are passed away; behold, all things have become new" (2 Corinthians 5:17). At your conversion, God made you an entirely new creation.

The authority of sin is dead in your life, because Jesus came as the Lamb to, "take away the sin of the world" (John 1:29). The sin of the world has been paid for in the finished work, and you and I are dead to the power of sin due to that work.

Since we have had the old man crucified and are alive in the Spirit, with Jesus residing inside of our hearts, the destiny of God can now take shape. Remember, He wants us to be conformed to the image of His Son (Romans 8:29).

The Greek word for "conformed" is *summorphos,* which means "to be made like unto." We derive the English word "morph" from this idea of being made like something else. The word "image" is the Greek word *eikon,* which means "copy, representation, or resemblance." God's destiny for us is that we be made like a copy or representation of Jesus.

How can God bring about such a thing? We have already established that we can't do it, and if it is going to be done, He is going to have to do it. I assume that if you disagreed with that assumption, you would have closed this book sometime ago. The fact that you are still reading tells me you know you can't change yourself, and you are beginning to believe that God's destiny for you is somehow wrapped up in Jesus Christ.

Paul used the Greek word "summorphos" in Romans to show our transformation, but in his second letter to Corinth, he chose a different route, showing us a depth of change that transcends anything we have ever seen.

"But we all, with unveiled face, beholding as in a mirror the glory of the Lord, are being transformed into the same image from glory to glory, just as by the Spirit of the Lord" (2 Corinthians 3:18).

The word "eikon" makes a comeback here, as Paul again speaks of us being made like a copy or representation of Jesus, but we see the word "changed" here as well. The Greek word used here is *metamorphoo,* from which we obviously derive the word "metamorphosis." The Greek word means "to transform or transfigure," and it is the same word used to describe what happens to Jesus in Matthew.

"And was *transfigured* before them. His face shone like the sun, and His clothes became as white as the light" (Matthew 17:2).

On the Mount of Transfiguration, Jesus' inner glory shined forth onto the outside. Peter, James, and John could see the "inner" Jesus, as He who hung the stars was appearing before them in that same glory. What a sight to see!

Imagine taking a sock and turning it inside out, with the stitches now showing where they had been hidden. Transfiguration was Jesus revealing on the surface who He had always been on the inside: a turning inside out, of sorts. The moment was brief but so powerful it prompted the voice of God to boom from heaven, "This is My beloved Son, in whom I am well pleased. Hear Him!" (Matthew 17:5).

When the glory of God appeared in the transfigured Jesus, men became amazed (verse 4), Moses (Law) and Elijah (Prophets) vanished (verse 8), and God spoke approvingly. When you and I allow the glory of God that rests in us to transform us into His image, the world will be amazed, the law and the prophets will not govern us, and God says He is, "Well pleased." Hallelujah! Good!

The only logical reason for Paul to use the word "metamorphoo" is if he thought the believer already contained inside of his heart the very thing that he needs to change his life. Paul doesn't tell us to go find that which transforms us, or to work harder at becoming better, but he references something already alive within us. He believed in a transformation of the believer, where who you are on the surface is slowly replaced by who you are inside. This transformation was not immediate, but it was certainly definite, and the Apostle Paul believed in it.

To make this transformation begin, Paul said that we behold the glory of the Lord, "as in a mirror" (2 Corinthians 3:18), meaning that Paul was telling us to look in the mirror in order to kick-start the transformation process. Of course, the phrase "as in a mirror" doesn't mean a literal mirror. What good would that do us? Good!

Notice that what we are actually beholding is "the glory of the Lord," with the analogy being that we should view His glory as if we are looking into a mirror. This is difficult for us to comprehend, as we imagine that looking into a mirror would show us all of our faults and failures. Paul is, once again, trying to reinforce who you really are, instead of what is showing up in your life. The more you gaze at His glory, the more the reflection should change to resemble Him.

On into the fourth chapter of 2 Corinthians, Paul explains to us exactly where we will find God's glory (remember, Paul didn't break the book into chapters, the translators did, thus it is all one, continuous thought by the author).

"For it is the God who commanded light to shine out of darkness, who has shone in our hearts to give the light of the knowledge of the glory of God in the face of Jesus Christ" (2 Corinthians 4:6).

Wow!

As we behold the face of Jesus, the knowledge of God's glory shines brighter in our hearts. If that is the case, the face that we should be looking at in that "mirror" is the face of Jesus. As the light turns on Jesus, lifting Him and bringing Him glory, we receive the benefits of change!

86

Honestly, that seems too good to be true. God put all of our sins into Christ and then punished them in Him through the death of the cross. Then, He placed the Holy Spirit into our hearts through our faith in that finished work. As if that isn't enough, the process of change then begins to take place by the power of the Spirit resting in us, with Him doing the work while we get the benefits. Our role in this process is to see more and more of Jesus and His loveliness. Our knowledge of God's glory grows leaps and bounds.

We can look at the finished work of Christ with no fear that it will ever lose its luster or its beauty. Remember that Paul said we now behold Him, "with unveiled face" (2 Corinthians 3:18). That phrase harkens back to the veil Moses placed over his face when he came down off Mount Sinai with the Ten Commandments. Moses put the veil there to hide the glory of God from the onlookers. We have no such veil, so does that mean our glory isn't as real as his? Or does it mean that we shouldn't hide his glory? Actually, the answer is neither.

"But if the ministry of death, written and engraved on stones, was glorious, so that the children of Israel could not look steadily at the face of Moses because of the glory of his countenance, which glory was passing away, how will the ministry of the Spirit not be more glorious?" (2 Corinthians 3:7, 8)

Paul calls that which is written and engraved on stones the "ministry of death." The only thing in the Bible that was written and engraved on stones was the Ten Commandments, thus Paul is stating that these moral laws, though just, holy, and good (Romans 7:12), could only minister death to the user, for they held no power to bring life.

There was glory on the moral law, but that "glory was to be done away." The contrast to that fading glory is the "ministry of the Spirit," which we know to be the work of the Holy Spirit under the New Covenant. Paul calls it "rather glorious," meaning the glory that is found in the message of grace and New Covenant is more glorious than that found in the law and the Old Testament.

That still doesn't explain to us why Moses put the veil over his face. Nor does it help us to figure out what Paul meant when he said that we behold God's glory with "open face." As we proceed further, however, we learn a shocking thing about Moses and God's glory.

"Unlike Moses, who put a veil over his face so that the children of Israel could not look steadily at the end of what was passing away" (2 Corinthians 3:13).

Did you catch it? Moses put the veil over his face so the children of Israel wouldn't notice that the glory was already fading! He simply wanted the luster to remain on the law as long as possible, since it was all that they had to live by. Paul calls the ministry of righteousness, "the glory that excelleth" (3:10), since he felt that the message of grace would never lose its luster.

Many people still read the Old Testament with the veil of protection over their hearts (3:15), unable to see that the glory has faded. They read of an angry God, pouring out vengeance and threats against His people, and they preach and teach it as if it is still to come upon God's church. There is no true liberty in their lives, for they are always in fear and trembling, never able to relax in the love of their Father. If we turn our hearts to the glory of the New Covenant, that veil will be ripped away, and we will know the liberty that Paul wrote about next.

"Now the Lord is the Spirit; and where the Spirit of the Lord is, there is liberty" (2 Corinthians 3:17).

Now that you are armed with the context that led to the powerful eighteenth verse, can you see that there is no reason for you to ever see God as a minister of vengeance and death again? I hope you can see that, as well as the fact that all of the transformation that needs to take place in your life will happen as you are effortlessly transformed into His image by feeding on the finished work of Christ.

The alternative to this is to look into the mirror at your own works. James speaks of this when he talks about people being hearers of the Word but not doers.

"For if anyone is a hearer of the word and not a doer, he is like a man observing his natural face in a mirror; for he observes himself, goes away, and immediately forgets what kind of man he was" (James 1:23, 24).

It sounds like James is talking about someone looking into the mirror and then, later in the day, forgetting what he looks like. How could this have anything to do with reading the Word, and what kind of person forgets what he looks like? The Greek phrase for "what kind of man" is *hopoios,* which means "what sort or quality." This man doesn't forget what he looks like; he forgets what quality of man he is! Looking at God's Word and then not applying it to your life is the starting point for forgetting who you are in Christ. Further, looking into the Word and not seeing Jesus will always cause you to forget what sort or quality of believer you are. How many times do we read and study the Word and never search for the loveliness of Jesus in those Old Testament verses? When we do this, we are cheating ourselves of the growth that is promised through the finished work.

"How do we find Jesus in the Old Testament? Isn't His life recorded in the New Testament?"

The life of Christ is recorded in the Gospels, which are the first four books of the New Testament, but that isn't where He began. He has been here from the beginning (John 1:1) and was manifested in human flesh so that He could accomplish God's plan for man's redemption (John 1:14). If you search the Scriptures, you can find Jesus all throughout the Word, standing in the shadows so that His appearance on earth could be the substance.

Jesus Himself taught us to teach and preach this way when He encountered two disciples on the road to Emmaus on the morning of His resurrection. He blinded their eyes from realizing that they were talking to Jesus and, instead, revealed Himself to them using the Scriptures.

> "And beginning at Moses and all the Prophets, He expounded to them in all the Scriptures the things concerning Himself" (Luke 24:27).

Jesus used the Old Testament to reveal Himself to these disciples, giving us both the permission and the commission to do the same. He was ripping off the veil from the Old Testament, showing us that the glory of the law had faded and that it was henceforth and forevermore, all about Jesus! This is why Paul said that the veil, "is taken away in Christ" (2 Corinthians 3:14).

When James finished his statement about looking into the Word and only seeing ourselves, he instructed us how to do it right. Notice how similar that James' statement is to what Paul told us in 2 Corinthians 3:18:

> "But he who looks into the perfect law of liberty and continues in it, and is not a forgetful hearer but a doer of the work, this one will be blessed in what he does" (James 1:25).

The "work" that James is talking about is what Paul told us as well. You and I are to find the glory of God in the face of Jesus. Our only "work" is to keep dwelling on just how finished the finished work actually is.

As our spirit-man concentrates more and more on Christ's finished work, there is not only an effortless transformation that takes place but an unconscious growth as well. Just as the fruit tree produces the fruit without effort, you and I produce His righteous acts. The tree also grows taller and wider, covering more ground with its shade and protection, and the believer grows stronger and more capable, as he feasts on His loveliness.

Jesus compared the Kingdom of God in us with a man who plants a seed in the ground and then goes about his daily business while the seed begins to flourish. Soon, the earth shoots forth a plant, then a bud, and then a finished product. The man does nothing to make it happen, but he is quick to harvest the fruit once it arrives (Mark 4:26–29). We are that man, and effortless transformation is happening in us in the same way it is happening in that parable. I want you to see the one thing that the story describes is the responsibility of the man:

> "And should sleep by night and rise by day, and the seed should sprout and grow, he himself does not know how" (Mark 4:27).

He only needs to sleep, and the seed does what it is designed to do. We must learn to rest in the finished work of Christ, while He does the work inside of us. We sleep. He works. We reap the harvest. Wow!

God's Final Step in Changing Man

The final step in God's plan for changing us into the image of His Son is to have Christ live through us, daily. Paul said that we are, "complete in Him" (Colossians 2:10), and John added, "As He is, so are we in this world" (1 John 4:17). If these Scriptures are true, they need no addition on our part. Christ living inside of us becomes an indisputable fact, which happens whether we know it or not. However, as we have seen, how much latitude is given to the Holy Spirit in our lives to bring the fruit out in our daily walk is directly proportional to how much we see the work as a finished work in Jesus Christ.

Interference on our part simply stunts the process of change. We are instructed to behold the face of Jesus and allow the Holy Spirit to change us. We have need of patience so that after we have accepted Christ as Savior, we might receive all of the promises of Christianity (Hebrews 10:36).

"Are you saying that I should just do nothing and expect the Holy Spirit to do the work?"

In short, yes! We will go deeper into your role in an upcoming chapter dedicated entirely to the obligation of Christians under the New Covenant. However, based on what we have already brought out, be quick to recognize that you are His righteousness, especially when you fail (2 Corinthians 5:21). Even though you may not see the fruit of the Spirit on display in your life, if you have accepted Christ as your Savior, continue to believe that His work is a finished work, and you are what the Bible says you are. If you have forgotten what it says, dig into its pages again. Remember the verses that have been covered here, and rest in their promises (2 Corinthians 5:21; Colossians 2:10; 1 John 4:17). Repeat !

"Pastor Paul, Jesus said that we should take up our cross and follow Him daily. That means we need to crucify our old man every day, right?"

Great question! That statement by Jesus caused me much confusion when I first began to understand the message of grace through the finished work of the cross. I heard it quoted over and over and even became convinced I needed a daily crucifixion to finish off my old nature.

The more I heard that message, the more wrapped up in works I became. I was encouraged to "concentrate on the cross" and remember that my victory was in "the cross, the cross, the cross." The ministries that were leading me this way were well intentioned, but many roads to bondage are paved with such intentions! I needed help, and perhaps you do, too.

Let's look at what Jesus said and the context in which He said it. Remember, context is everything, for nothing is said independent of the surrounding verses.

"'If anyone desires to come after Me, let him deny himself, and take up his cross daily, and follow me'" (Luke 9:23).

Now, let's compare that statement to something said by the Apostle Paul.

"Knowing this, that our old man was crucified with Him, that the body of sin might be done away with, that we should no longer be slaves of sin … For the death that He died, He died to sin once for all; but the life that He lives, He lives to God. Likewise you also, reckon yourselves to be dead indeed to sin, but alive to God in Christ Jesus our Lord" (Romans 6:6, 10, 11).

Paul made a few things very clear:

1. Our old nature has been crucified with Christ, destroying sin's influence, setting us free.

2. Jesus died on the cross *one* time, but His resurrected life is eternal.

3. Consider yourself dead in the same manner that Jesus was and, likewise, alive the same way.

We can determine from these points that we are dead to sin in the same manner that Jesus is. Did He die multiple times? If He died once, and we should consider ourselves dead in the same way, how many times should we die to sin? Once!

Then, what did Jesus mean when He told His disciples to take up the cross daily?

When Jesus made that statement, Calvary had yet to occur. To His disciples, the cross was simply a Roman instrument of death: the final destination for criminals and enemies. For Jesus to reference the death of the cross, He had to be referencing a physical death, which the context of the next few verses bears out.

> "For whoever desires to save his life will lose it, but whoever loses his life for My sake, will save it ... But I tell you truly, there are some standing here who shall not taste death till they see the kingdom of God" (Luke 9:24, 27).

If Jesus intended for His listeners to take up their spiritual cross every day, why does He immediately change the subject to martyrdom and close by prophesying to them that some of them would see Him in His glory without tasting death? (By the way, that prophesy was fulfilled in the next few verses, when Jesus revealed the glory of transfiguration to Peter, James, and John.)

To the disciples who heard it, Christ's instruction to take up the cross every day would have meant they should be ready every single day to lay down their lives for His cause. This should mean the same to us today. Those of us who can't do that have already lost our lives anyway (Luke 9:24).

"But didn't the Apostle Paul confirm this when he said, 'I die daily?'"

Paul did say, "I die daily," but look at the verses in front of it and behind it.

"And why do we stand in jeopardy every hour? I affirm, by the boasting in you which I have in Christ Jesus our Lord, *I die daily*. If, in the manner of men, I have fought with beasts at Ephesus, what advantage is it to me? If the dead do not rise, 'Let us eat and drink, for tomorrow we die!'" (1 Corinthians 15:30–32).

It is plain to see that Paul is talking about the physical perils he faces in ministry. His sermon is dealing with resurrection, as it has been since the twelfth verse of this chapter. In light of the constant threats against his physical body, standing so close to death as to be near it daily, what good is it if there is no hope of eternal life? His daily death isn't to his old nature or to sin's power over him. His daily death was the threat that today might be his last!

God Did the Work; Man Reaped the Reward

Adam, in the Garden of Eden, is a perfect picture of the finished work. Adam had no sin, and he was made in the very likeness and image of God. God did all of the work, leaving Adam only with the task of dressing and keeping the Garden (Genesis 2:15). What did Adam get out of this deal? He was given permission to eat of every tree in the Garden except the Tree of Knowledge of Good and Evil (Genesis 2:16). Notice that God did all of the creating, while Adam did all of the guarding. By guarding the finished work of the Garden, he reaped the benefits.

There were no thorns or weeds to contend with in Eden until after the fall of man. As soon as man began living by his efforts (Knowledge of Good and Evil), he was doomed to do more than just tend the Garden; now he was responsible to make everything grow. He actually went from *guarding* to *gardening,* as God instructed him to, "till the ground" (Genesis 3:23). Now that Christ has died and restored us to a state similar to that of Adam in Eden, we go back to guarding His work.

Guarding the finished work will keep you from some Christians' most common pastime: fighting the devil. Believer, stop trying to defeat Satan! He is already a defeated foe (Hebrews 2:14; 1 John 3:8). Simply show the defeat of Satan by recognizing that defeat at Calvary. When he attacks you, he does so as a lion that roars while on the prowl (1 Peter 5:8). What kind of lion roars before he makes the kill? The only reason the devil is making so much noise in your life is that he knows he is defeated. Scaring you to death has become his only option.

Enforce the finished work when you face the enemy. Remind him of the defeat that he experienced when Christ took all of your sins into His body and suffered for you. As you do this, you will stop striving *for* victory and start fighting *from* victory. There is a big difference, believer, as you already know.

Enforcement of the finished work of Christ is not screaming out Scriptures and gritting our teeth in concentrated effort. Due to what we know about the cross and what Jesus has done to change our insides, let's stop confessing to *have* and start confessing because we *already have.*

What exactly do we have? Let's be reminded.

"In whom we have redemption through His blood, the forgiveness of sins" (Colossians 1:14).

"In Him we have redemption through His blood, the forgiveness of sins, according to the riches of His grace" (Ephesians 1:7).

I am all for the practice of confessing but not just to any old thing that comes to mind. Let's confess what the Bible says about who we really are, not just what is showing up. We should use our faith to believe in the finished work of Christ, not just to avoid things that we don't want. Even those who have little knowledge of anything else in the Bible can begin resting in the finished work the moment they have a revelation of how marvelous it is.

Always Look for Favor!

Ruth the Moabitess was the product of a heathen, idol-worshipping nation that sacrificed their own children to a golden god. The widow of a Hebrew man, she returned to the city of Bethlehem with her mother-in-law in the book that bears her name. Look at her confession, and remember that if a heathen with no knowledge of God can confess such goodness, how much more can you and I, who are joint heirs with Jesus, believe in God for good things?

"So Ruth the Moabitess said to Naomi, 'Please let me go to the field and glean heads of grain after him in whose sight I may find favor'" (Ruth 2:2).

She went looking for God's grace and trusted that even though she was undeserving, someone would have favor on her. The man that found her was Boaz, a type of Jesus, who buys her as his own, just as Jesus did for us. This "unbeliever" believed God for favor, and God responded!

Boaz decides to marry Ruth, but he is hindered by a Jewish statute that demands the nearest relative to her dead husband have first rights to all of his properties, including his wife. Boaz is next in line after this particular man, so he goes through the proper ceremony to purchase Ruth as his own. This story is given in beautiful detail in the fourth chapter of Ruth and concludes with the genealogy that came from Ruth and Boaz's union. Just before that, Ruth wonders what to do about the nearer kinsman, and her mother-in-law, Naomi, gives her priceless advice.

"Then she said, 'Sit still, my daughter, until you know how the matter will turn out; for the man will not rest until he has concluded the matter this day'" (Ruth 3:18).

You sit still, for the man will not rest until the work is finished! Jesus never cried, "It is finished," until He had done all that needed done at Calvary. He didn't rest so that you could always rest. Now, sit still, and let Jesus determine "how the matter will turn out."

Perhaps you are reading this book because you are looking for help, and the other self-help books didn't really help at all. Maybe the idea of "Revelation to Transformation" seemed a bit far-fetched but worth a shot, since no transformation was coming from all of your previous efforts. What separates what you are reading now from what you may have read before is that none of the self-help books of the world ever deal in the realm of God's favor. They deal with your "plan," but never with a complete confidence that God is going to be good and do good simply because you belong to Him. Of course, a worldly book on self-help wouldn't include references to you being children of God through the finished work of Christ, either!

We opened this chapter with a question, and I hope that we have answered it. Just how finished is the finished work of Christ? My prayer is that this chapter has opened your eyes to the all-encompassing power of the cross of Jesus Christ. May you move forward, secure in the knowledge that even though all of your problems haven't vanished and some of your issues keep resurfacing, there is more than meets the eye. Now, and forever more, may you see Christ as living inside of you as the hope of glory and know that He is the reason the fruit of the Spirit come out of us in the first place.

Now that we understand the role of the cross in our transformation, it is time to let the Holy Spirit go to work. He has been stirring to do His part in you since the moment you were converted. In the next chapter, we find out how He is activated and what He will do once He begins His part of the finished work. We will also learn what He does not do, which is as eye-opening as anything else we are about to learn.

Good Chapter

The Role of the Spirit | 9

"But we all, with open face beholding as in a glass the glory of the Lord, are changed into the same image from glory to glory, even as *by the Spirit of the Lord*" (2 Corinthians 3:18 KJV).

We open this chapter with a verse that we gleaned much truth from in the previous chapter. In that study, we learned what it meant to have "open face" and to behold Jesus in the mirror of God's Word. We also dealt with the transformation that happens as we see His finished work, with God turning us into what He wants us to be. Now we go further and place the emphasis on the final phrase, seeing that all of this occurs in us, "by the Spirit of the Lord."

It is the work of the Holy Spirit in us that ultimately changes us, and He does His work due to the fact that Jesus paid for our redemption. From the moment that He enters our heart at conversion, He functions in the role of Comforter, which also means He is our counselor (John 16:7). Use that definition of the Holy Spirit as a way to help you to understand whether the voice you are heeding is that of the Spirit or merely of your flesh (or even of the enemy). If what you hear does not sound like the wise advice of a counselor, reject it, as He must live up to His namesake.

The Convicting Power of the Holy Spirit

The term "conviction" is about as common in the church as the word "demon" or "rapture," so you may not be surprised to learn that it appears in the Bible precisely as many times as those two words. What you might find surprising is that number is zero! The word "conviction" never appears in the King James Version of the Bible, although its presence is most certainly felt.

To be fair, the word "convicted" does appear in the book of John, when Jesus tells those who are about to stone the woman caught in the act of adultery to go on and stone her if they have no sin of their own.

"And they which heard it, being convicted by their own conscience, went out one by one" (John 8:9).

We know that the Bible wasn't written in English, for as we have discussed before, the Old Testament was in Hebrew, and the New Testament was in Greek. To find how many times a word is really used, we must go back to the original language. In this case, the word used here for "convicted" is the Greek word *elenkho,* and means "to convict." This Greek word appears seventeen times in the New Testament, showing us that there is certainly a heavy emphasis placed on conviction in one form or the other.

The men in John 8 were obviously convicted, but what were they convicted by? The text said that they were convicted "by their own conscience," and knowing that these men were Jews who had knowledge of the law, their consciences told them they, too, had committed sin. They didn't need the Holy Spirit to convict them of their sin, because their own conscience did it for them. Right !

Where, then, does the Bible tell us the Holy Spirit convicts us of our sins? Would you be surprised if I told you that the Bible does not say that? I know it's shocking, but let's repeat it just so there is no misunderstanding. The Bible *never* says the Holy Spirit is here to convict us of our sins.

Most Bible students will quickly run to the closest verse they can find to refute our previous statement, and it will invariably be found in John 16. The Greek word that we used for "to convict" does appear in John 16, and it obviously means what we think it means. Watch the use and notice what the role of the Holy Spirit is in conviction:

Convict

"And when He [the Holy Spirit] is come, He will reprove the world of sin, and of righteousness, and of judgment" (John 16:8; brackets mine).

According to this statement by Jesus, the Holy Spirit obviously comes to reprove (convict) the world. The word "world" here does not denote worldliness as in sinners and unbelievers, but rather it is the word *kosmos,* meaning that the Holy Spirit is here to convict the human race as a whole.

The verse bears out that there are three distinct things of which the Holy Spirit will convict the world: sin, righteousness, and judgment. Each individual conviction has its own accompanying verse, and in these verses, we get a better understanding of what the Holy Spirit is actually here to do and why He is here to do it.

The Holy Spirit Convicts the World of Sin

"Of sin, because they do not believe in me" (John 16:9).

Jesus speaks specifically of the Holy Spirit's power to convict the world of sin, even directing His statement at a particular group of people. The use of the word "they" shows us that Jesus is pointing outside of His circle of listeners to reference the unbeliever. He was speaking to the disciples, but when He mentions conviction of sin, He looks beyond them to a world of people who have not placed faith in Jesus Christ.

The verse also shows that the Holy Spirit's conviction is against "sin" and not "sins." Since the word is singular, we know that the conviction is not against individual acts of sin but one particular sin. To solve the mystery as to what sin Jesus is referring to, we need to understand the possible options.

1. "Sin"—As the nature of man, passed from our first father Adam down through the human race. This references sin as a whole.

2. "Sin"—As in one particular sin, denoting this one sin is the worst sin of all and placing it above all others.

On first glance, we might automatically assume that Jesus is referencing the first definition of "sin," meaning that the Holy Spirit is here to convict the world of the sin nature inside of them. However, in light of other Scriptures, this cannot be the case. For example, John the Baptist said of Jesus, "Behold! The Lamb of God who takes away the sin of the world!" (John 1:29) The "sin of the world" is singular here as well, meaning that Jesus came to release man from the power of the sin nature that dwells in him due to the sin of Adam. If that be the case, the Holy Spirit would be wasting His time in convicting sinners of the nature of sin in their hearts, since Jesus died to that sin and for that sin (Romans 7:10).

That must mean that the second definition of "sin" is the one for which the Holy Spirit is convicting the world. There must be one particular sin that He is constantly dealing with in the heart of a sinner.

99

Could this particular sin be murder, or adultery, or lust? What one sin is so big that the Holy Spirit would confine all of His conviction to it? Jesus said it one way, and John the Baptist said it another.

"For God did not send His Son into the world to condemn the world, but that the world through Him might be saved. He who believes in Him is not condemned; but he who does not believe is condemned already, because he has not believed in the name of the only begotten Son of God" (John 3:17, 18).

"He who believes in the Son has everlasting life; and he who does not believe the Son shall not see life, but the wrath of God abides on him" (John 3:36).

The one sin that places man under condemnation and wrath is the sin of unbelief. Because Jesus has died to take away the sin of the world, men cannot go to hell over the things that they do. Instead, men miss heaven over the one thing they never do: accept Jesus Christ by faith. This is the sin Jesus says will be the source of the Holy Spirit's conviction on the world, "'because they believe not on me.'"

The Holy Spirit Convicts the World of Righteousness

"'Of righteousness, because I go to My Father and you see me no more'" (John 16:10).

The second conviction that is brought on by the Holy Spirit is the conviction of righteousness. If this verse applies to the unbeliever, the first conviction doesn't make much sense, as there is no righteousness in an unbeliever. Can you guess to whom this verse is directed?

Jesus turns His sermon inward now, toward the audience of the disciples. The phrase, "you see me no more," means that this conviction will be aimed at those who already know Christ and are declared to be His righteousness. In other words, this verse is directed at the church!

Paul declared that you and I are the righteousness of God in Christ, due to Christ being made sin for all of us (2 Corinthians 5:21). He also stated that the believer should wake up to his righteousness, which will lead to an end of sin (1 Corinthians 15:34). We are righteous based on no works of our own, yet our lifestyles don't always show forth this right-standing. Due to the fact that Jesus does not walk and talk with us physically, it is often easy for us to forget just how righteous we are. This is where the Holy Spirit's conviction comes into play.

Jesus knew He was going to ascend into heaven and that the disciples (as well as you and me) were going to have to run this race alone. However, He knew that the accompanying counsel of the Holy Spirit would be enough inside of us to help us along the way. This is why He states that the Spirit will constantly convict us of our righteousness, due to the fact that our faith is so easily shaken on a day-to-day basis.

Can you understand why I say that the Holy Spirit is not in you to convict you of sin? He is actually in you to convict, or to "convince" you that you are righteous all of the time. We must learn to heed to the voice of the Spirit in this area and be quick to declare our righteousness, especially when we don't feel like it. When we do this, we are lining up with what the Holy Spirit says about us.

"Pastor, even if this is correct, isn't it all pretty much the same thing? I mean, when you mess up, the Holy Spirit comes along and convicts you of it. Whether He is convicting you of the act of sin or of your righteousness, what does it matter? He's still convicting you, right?"

I pose this particular question because that argument has been raised regarding these passages of Scripture. However, I strongly disagree that it is the same thing. If these two are one in the same, the only way to have the Holy Spirit reinforce your righteousness is for you to fail. Based on the nature of the question, conviction would only be attached to sin and is something that should always make you have an emotional response.

Unfortunately, our idea of conviction is linked directly with sin. In other words, we think that if there is conviction, it is because we have done something wrong. Yet, Jesus declares that only one in three times that the Holy Spirit is convicting, does it have anything to do with sin at all. Recall that the text declares the Holy Spirit convicts of "sin", "righteousness" and "judgment". Again, of the three things He convicts of, only one is "sin". Jesus didn't say, "He will convict you of righteousness because you just sinned and you need to be reminded of who you are." When He convicts the believer, it is to remind him of his right-standing. Granted, this can and does happen when a believer fails, but it most certainly is not isolated to that moment.

Some of our erroneous thinking is tied to our insistence that people who fail show some sort of emotional response when they get things right. We want them to cry, hang their head, or go through some ritual of repentance. We might not be all that happy with the Prodigal Son, for when he came back to his father, the Scripture never even has him saying, "I'm sorry!" The father knew his heart and was glad to have him back home. Only the elder brother was upset by the party atmosphere of his return.

The day-by-day battle of living for Christ is going to bring countless challenges. We will feel temptations, trials, struggles, discouragement, and sometimes we will even feel all alone. We constantly need the solid voice of reinforcement in our hearts to remind us of how much we are loved and how we are viewed in the eyes of the Father due to the presence of Jesus in our hearts. Because Jesus went to the Father, and we can't see Him with our eyes, it is going to be easy to feel like He isn't with us at all. The Holy Spirit is here to convince us that He is still here, and we are still who the Bible says we are!

This point should be hammered home, because far too many pulpits tend to leave the Holy Spirit at the doorstep of the sinner, pointing out all of his sins. Even with a proper understanding of what the Spirit is actually convicting sinners of, we continue to insult His office by assuming that He is still dealing with the believer over the same issues. The Spirit has moved on to His second role, and that is of "Reinforcer of our Righteousness."

How does the Holy Spirit reinforce our righteousness? Even if we know that He is convicting us of who we are in Christ, it is important to know in what manner He will do it so that we will quickly recognize His work when we see it. Let's list some of the ways the Holy Spirit convicts the believer of righteousness.

1. *He tells us we are loved.*

What an underappreciated role of the Holy Spirit! The first time Paul mentions the Holy Spirit, in the great book of Romans, it is in relation to the love of God: "Now hope does not disappoint, because the love of God has been poured in our hearts by the Holy Spirit who was given to us" (Romans 5:5). Of all of the things Paul could have listed as jobs of the Holy Spirit, the very first one is to show the believer that the Spirit is always reminding you that you are loved. Thank God for this blessed gift!

2. He witnesses to us of the details of the finished work.

We hear sermons on how we should witness to others about Jesus, but how many have you heard on how the Holy Spirit is constantly witnessing to you? The author of Hebrews declared that one of the jobs of the Holy Spirit is to be a witness to what He saw at Calvary. He watched Christ suffer and die, and He now relates that in the heart of the redeemed.

> "But the Holy Spirit also witnesses to us; for after He had said before, 'This is the covenant that I will make with them after those days, says the LORD: I will put My laws into their hearts, and in their minds I will write them,' then He adds, 'Their sins and their lawless deeds I will remember no more'" (Hebrews 10:15–17).

The Holy Spirit witnesses to us of the finished work and of the things that God has said. Did you notice that one of those things is to remind the believer that God doesn't remember his sins and his iniquities? Wow!

If the Holy Spirit convicts us of our sins, how can He also convince us that God no longer remembers our sins? These two convictions cannot exist together. For the Holy Spirit to find our sin, He would have to circumvent the blood of Jesus and basically ignore the finished work altogether. When we say that the Holy Spirit doesn't convict us of our sins, we are not ignoring the fact that we fail, and we are not making sin seem insignificant. Rather, we refuse to insult the office of the Holy Spirit and act as if the Spirit and the Son are working against each another. By emphasizing your righteousness, the Spirit isn't going soft on sin: He is honoring the finished work.

John said, "the blood of Jesus Christ ... cleanses us from all sin" (1 John 1:7). The Greek syntax here denotes a constant cleansing, not just a one-time event. The blood of Jesus is always working, just like the blood on the doors of the Hebrews in the land of Egypt. Come wind or rain, the blood was still there, and redemption was found in the blood.

"But doesn't John go on to say if we confess our sins that He is faithful and just to forgive us? Doesn't this mean that we should confess all of them, and if we don't, there is no forgiveness? It sounds like the cleansing power of the blood isn't automatic but depends on confession."

I will admit that when read by itself, with no context used, this Scripture does sound like there is no forgiveness without confession. But we both know the Bible can't be read that way.

John told us in verse 3 that he is writing these things so, "ye also may have fellowship with us," meaning that these next verses are aimed at someone who doesn't walk in fellowship with believers. He then tells him that if he claims to have no sin, he is a liar. Does this sound like a message that should be delivered to believers? No! These are unbelievers, who deny they even need a Savior. Yet John tells them that if they confess their sins, they will be made righteous as well.

When John opens the second chapter, he turns his attention to the believer, addressing him as "My little children" and then assuring him that if he sins, "we have an Advocate with the Father, Jesus Christ the righteous" (1 John 2:1). Be assured if you sin, your advocate goes to work on your behalf, for He is the, "propitiation [satisfaction] *for our sins*" (1 John 2:2, brackets mine).

If confession of your sins is necessary to receive forgiveness, there can be no exception to that rule. You would have to confess every single thing that you did, or thought, or said that was wrong. You would even have to confess the things you didn't do but should have done!

I remember asking someone about this when I was a child, wondering whether I would go to hell if I missed confessing something during my time of prayer. The response was, "Well, God's grace would cover those." All I could think was, *What? If grace covers the one I forget about, why not forget about all of them, so I'm certain to be covered by God's grace?* My line of thinking was very immature, but can you see why I thought that? Constant confession places an emphasis on sin, rather than on the Savior, and it puts you in charge of changing you. Life becomes very confusing once *you* take hold of the reins of your transformation.

3. *He makes Jesus look glorious.*

"'He will glorify Me, for He will take of what is Mine and declare it to you'" (John 16:14).

Jesus makes this statement just after our key text, in a group of verses that show what the Holy Spirit will be here to accomplish. Whatever He does will always bring glory to Jesus, or as I like to say it, He will make Jesus look glorious. The word "glory" is the Greek word *doksazo*, which means "to praise, magnify, or render excellent."

4. He shines a light on our perfect standing.

The Holy Spirit will always shine light in our lives that will bring glory to Jesus and reemphasize our standing in Christ. He shines on the same things that Jesus shines on, and Jesus declared Himself to be, "'the light of the world'" (John 8:12).

Have you ever considered the scenario that Jesus was in when He called Himself the "'light of the world'"? What an amazing statement to make in the first place! It is even more amazing when we learn that He did it twice, in back-to-back chapters, and both times followed a mighty revelation in someone's life.

The first time He said it is preceded by this verse, spoken to the woman caught in the act of adultery: "'Neither do I condemn you; go and sin no more'" (John 8:11). The moment Jesus gives the sinful woman the beautiful gift of no condemnation, He declares Himself to be the light of the world. From there on, the light of the world is only revealed to shine light on the fact that you have no condemnation. Can you see the connection? He doesn't declare Himself to be the light to reveal hidden sins or to show up people. The light of Christ is always shining in your heart to convince you that you are His righteousness.

He uses it again in John 9, when He and the disciples meet a man who has been blind from birth. The disciples ask whether his own sin or his parents' sin has made him blind, and Jesus answered that it had nothing to do with sin. No doubt, this young man had wondered the same thing in his heart many times before this fateful day, and Jesus declared the answer to free the man from guilt and condemnation. Only then could the young man receive the healing that he so desired. However, just before he was healed, and just after his spirit had been set free from guilt, Jesus declared, "'As long as I am in the world, I am the light of the world'" (John 9:5). Again, Christ shines light on our perfect standing in the Father.

"But doesn't the Bible say that God searches the hearts? If He is searching, what is He looking for if not hidden sin?"

First of all, if God has to search the hearts to find hidden sin, He isn't as all-knowing as we think He is! How could you hide your sin from an all-seeing God? That debunks the "hidden sin" theory, which tries to explain the convicting power of the Holy Spirit.

105

Second, the Bible does indeed say that He searches the heart. Look at the whole verse with the verse that leads into it, and we will find another way that the Holy Spirit reinforces our righteousness.

5. *He intercedes on our behalf.*

"Now He who searches the hearts knows what the mind of the Spirit is, because He makes intercession for the saints according to the will of God" (Romans 8:27).

The searching of the hearts is done by God, because the Holy Spirit is interceding on our behalf. The Holy Spirit is acting as a "go-between" between us and the Lord, helping with the things we don't even know we need help with. Due to the work of the Holy Spirit, the Father can look deep into our hearts and work change in the darkest areas.

God knows your heart better than you do! We forget who we are in Christ due to our circumstances, but the Holy Spirit in us never forgets. Jesus asked Peter, "'Simon, do you love me?'" to which Peter responded, "'Yes Lord, you know I love you'" (John 21:16). This disciple, who just denied he even knew the Lord, is no doubt answering in a way that leans on the knowledge of the Lord more than on his own. In effect, Peter was saying, "Lord, you know me better than I do."

John, who was witness to that conversation between Peter and Jesus, wrote this in his first epistle: "For if our heart condemns us, God is greater than our heart, and knows all things" (1 John 3:20). Even if I condemn myself, God is smarter than I, and He knows the truth about me. Hallelujah!

The Holy Spirit Convicts the World of Judgment

"Of judgment, because the prince of this world is judged" (John 16:11 KJV).

The final conviction of the Holy Spirit toward the world regards judgment, and it is wholly involved with the idea that the prince of this world is judged. This *does not* point to the future judgment of the world or to the devil, for it is spoken as a done deal. Jesus uses this statement to solidify something that he said four chapters prior.

"Now is the judgment of this world; now the ruler of this world will be cast out" (John 12:31).

God's judgment against the sin of the world happened at the cross, with Satan (the prince of this world) being cast out of the position of authority and power. After the cross and the resurrection, Jesus would state, "'All authority has been given to Me in heaven and on earth'" (Matthew 28:18). With sin judged and Satan rendered powerless, the Holy Spirit goes about convicting (or convincing) the world of this fact. I like to categorize these three convictions this way:

- Holy Spirit's dealings with the sinner (John 16:9)

- Holy Spirit's dealings with the saint (John 16:10)

- Holy Spirit's dealings with Satan (John 16:11)—for even the devil needs reminded that He has lost

I hope you don't find that last statement strange, because, yes, even the devil needs to be reminded he has been defeated. When Christ died at Calvary, He nailed the law to the cross and then showed that victory to Satan and his forces (Colossians 2:14–15). Read.
The Holy Spirit also wants to remind you and me that our enemy has been defeated. We have nothing to fear with regards to the devil, for he is powerless to touch the child of God that is at rest in the finished work. The author of Hebrews said that through His death, Jesus destroyed, "him that had the power of death, that is, the devil" (Hebrews 2:14). The Greek for "destroy" is *katargeo*, which means "to render idle, unemployed, inactive, to cause to have no further efficiency." Good,
Saint, be reminded of that last sentence over and over again. Jesus' death at Calvary has rendered Satan unemployed and caused him to have no further efficiency. Any efficient employment on his part must be provided by our refusal to rest in the lovely, finished work of our Lord Jesus Christ. May the Holy Spirit convince us of this truth!
This process of transformation is entirely the work of the Holy Spirit, who works through the finished work of Jesus Christ. We are the beneficiaries of His perfect work, as we see Him changing and transforming us daily. He reinforces our righteousness by reiterating the truths of the New Covenant to us, by reminding us that we are deeply loved, by making Jesus appear lovely, by shining a light on our right-standing, and by interceding to the Father for our deepest needs.

After all of this, it is *finally* time to see what our individual role is in the process of transformation. We all want to do something to "help the Holy Spirit," but we have learned that this only hinders. Don't worry, we are not going to change our tune now and inject a chapter full of formulas or works into your Christian experience. Instead, we are going to use God's Word to teach you an important truth about yourself. Armed with this truth, you will be ready to do the only thing that you can possibly do to see permanent change.

Good Chapter!

Our Role in Transformation | 10

As we brought out in the final paragraphs of the previous chapter, Satan has been rendered unemployed due to the finished work of Christ. Any opportunity for employment he now has must be at the expense of the believer, due to our ignorance of just how finished the finished work is. This means that what we know is of extreme importance, and what we do with that knowledge can mean the difference between liberty and bondage.

I hope you have seen how useless and ineffectual all of our works and human efforts are in transforming us into His image. Not only can we make no permanent change, we have shown that we can actually stunt our own growth and development by interfering with the transformation process that has begun within us by the Holy Spirit.

When I was boy, I remember hearing an evangelist make a statement that stayed with me for years. He said that we should always be careful how we pray, because we just might get what we ask for—and it might not be all that we thought it would be. He used a sample prayer, stating, "Lord, let me see me as you see me." He went on to preach how, not long after praying that prayer, the Lord had shown him his filth and pride and other areas of sin that he didn't even know were there. He preached it with such passion and fire, and I remember being emotionally moved.

Not knowing better, I began to incorporate that evangelist's prayer into my own prayer life, praying it for myself, hoping to have God reveal to me all of the hidden things that needed purged from my heart. Anything that happened in the subsequent days or weeks after I prayed that prayer, I linked back to that moment and began to believe that God was trying to teach me a lesson or to discipline me into submission.

One day, this time in adulthood, I distinctly remember the Lord speaking to me in response to that same prayer. I had just finished a time of being alone with God when I closed with my old, familiar refrain, "Lord, please let me see me the way you see me." I will never forget when He spoke into my heart, "Son, if I let you see you the way I see you, you will only see the perfection of Jesus." Needless to say, I was stunned! Quickly, the Spirit brought Paul's writing to the church at Colosse to my heart, for only Scripture can confirm what the Lord says to us.

"For ye are dead, and your life is hidden with Christ in God" (Colossians 3:3).

Believing I had heard the voice of God speaking in my heart, I dug deeper into this Scripture and was stunned to find that Paul was talking about each and every one of us. For some reason, I had that Scripture in my head as if Paul was speaking of himself, but there is no indication of this. This is a statement of fact by Paul about all believers. Having placed our faith in Christ, the old man inside of us is now considered to be "dead," and the life that we live is hidden inside of Christ. If God shows us who we really are, He can show us nothing but Jesus.

You can imagine how transformative this moment was for me, just as I hope that it is for some of you. However, one Scripture is never enough. I wanted more!

"I have been crucified with Christ; it is no longer I who live, but Christ lives in me; and the life which I now live in the flesh I live by faith in the Son of God, who loved me and gave Himself for me" (Galatians 2:20).

Again, it isn't you and me who are living; it is Christ who is living in and through us. I don't mean we aren't physically alive, for that is obviously not the case. I mean that we are not who we used to be, even if we occasionally act like we used to act. This is how God sees us.

I couldn't be condemned for praying that prayer for all of those years, and the evangelist who unwittingly taught me to do it had no malice in his instruction, for a person can only walk in the light that he is given. We can't be expected to know or understand the things we have never been taught, but once we have learned them, we have an obligation to apply them. As light is coming into the areas in your life that you have struggled with and questioned, you move into a realm where you should never be the same again.

The results this evangelist was seeing are not unlike what any of us will see when we focus our eyes on our sins and failures. If the heartbeat behind your prayer is to find sin, you will most certainly find sin. However, if your heart beats to find Jesus, you will see Him revealed as lovely. We cannot dispel darkness by removing darkness; we must insert light. Light has come into your darkness, and I believe that your darkness is in trouble!

"Pastor, I am trying to get my hands off of my transformation, but Jesus doesn't seem to be working!"

Don't fret! The mighty transformative power of the Holy Spirit is at work, and Jesus' finished work, works. Let's start our role in the process by having patience and allowing the Spirit to do His perfect work.

"For ye have need of patience, that, after ye have done the will of God, ye might receive the promise" (Hebrews 10:36 KJV).

Do you recall Jesus' parable of the sower who went forth sowing seed? He explained that the sower tossed the seed onto four types of ground: wayside, rocky, thorny, and good ground. The first three types of ground have their obvious problems in bringing forth fruit, but sowing seeds in good ground should work, simply by definition. Look at Christ's statement of exactly *how* that fruit will come forth.

"But the ones that fell on the good ground are those who, having heard the word with a noble and good heart, keep it and bear fruit with patience" (Luke 8:15).

The fruit of the Spirit will come forth; we must simply be patient, and let the seed do what God has designed it to do.

"But Pastor Paul, you don't understand, I have been patient. In fact, I have been patient for years, and I am still struggling with the same old things."

Fair enough, but now that you are being introduced (or reintroduced) to the power of the finished work, let's allow that knowledge to take root and work miracles in your life. Also, let's make sure that our minds are lined up perfectly with the mind of God. He thinks of you one way, so why not think the same way?

Change Your Mind

The Greek word for "repent" is *metanoeo*, which means "to change one's mind." Fundamentally, when a person is called to repentance, he is being asked to change his mind about something. He could be changing his mind about his own sinful state or even about how he views God.

Paul never called the church to "repentance" as it regarded their sins, but he certainly believed in a proper framework for repentance. It is proper to call for repentance in the event that our minds are not properly established in truth, so we may have them so established as to never have to change them again. Paul said, "For godly sorrow produces repentance leading to salvation, not to be regretted; but the sorrow of the world produces death" (2 Corinthians 7:10). In other words, there is a godly way to change your mind, and when you do that, you will have changed it for the last time!

Back in chapter 6, we briefly discussed Paul's habit of reinforcement, where he constantly appeals to the knowledge that the church should already have. Paul is simply reminding the believer of both who and what he is in Christ so that this knowledge will provide him with all that he needs. If our knowledge is right, our living will be right, or as I have heard that Charles Spurgeon once said, "Right believing leads to right living."

Remember how Paul told the church at Corinth they would be changed from glory to glory as they beheld the face of Jesus (2 Corinthians 3:18)? Paul returns to that same word for "transformed," which means that our outside should reflect our inside, when he addresses the church at Rome.

"And do not be conformed to this world, but be transformed by the renewing of your mind, that you may prove what is that good, and acceptable and perfect will of God" (Romans 12:2).

The Greek word for "conformed" in this passage means to pattern after a certain thing, which shows us that Paul thinks it's beneath a believer to pattern his or her lifestyle after the way a sinner might live. The opposite of this would be to have a transformation, where we change into something else. The fulfillment of that transformation is our Scripture in 2 Corinthians 3:18; but notice what we are supposed to do in the act of transformation: "Be transformed by the renewing of your mind."

I am not told to "repent" here, or to "change my mind." Rather, I am instructed to renew my mind, which is a renovation or a complete change for the better. I have heard the truth before, but I need to renovate the way I think so that I can see transformation come out in my life. All of the components are there; I just need to align my mind with His mind so that He can do His perfect work.

Any and all separation you might think exists between you and God has always been in your own mind. Satan functions so powerfully in the area of our mind, because it is the one place he can go to work with our help. When Paul explained to the church at Colossi that Christ had made peace through the blood of His cross and reconciled all things back to Himself, he personalized it, stating that they, too, were reconciled. However, he stated that prior to that reconciliation, "And you, who once were alienated and enemies in your mind by wicked works, yet now He has reconciled" (Colossians 1:21). The alienation wasn't on the part of God; it was in their minds, and it was due to the fact that they thought their wicked works was what separated them from God.

Believer, please remember that wicked works are not what separate men from God. Men are only separated from God by their lack of acceptance of the finished work of Jesus Christ. That isn't meant to condone wicked works; in fact, the acknowledgment that your works do not separate you from God's love will provide the power to stop doing the wicked works!

Think Like Jesus

You know that Jesus (who committed no sin) was made to be sin so that you (who committed no righteousness) could be made righteous. Because of this exchange, you and I have the promise that we are in complete in Christ (Colossians 2:10), perfected forever (Hebrews 10:14), and as He is, so are we in this world (1 John 4:17).

Faced with such an overwhelming mountain of scriptural proof that we are what the Bible says we are, it is high time that we line up our minds to think in the same manner. Paul said, "Let this mind be in you, which was also in Christ Jesus" (Philippians 2:5). Whatever the mind-set of Jesus was, we are encouraged to have the same thing.

We learn exactly what that mind-set was in the very next verse.

"Who, being in the form of God, *thought* it not robbery to be equal with God" (Philippians 2:6 KJV).

I emphasized the word "thought" to show you that verse 6 is telling us what mind was in Christ Jesus. Did you catch what His thoughts were? The phrase "thought it not robbery" is translated, "thought it not a thing to be grasped after," meaning that Jesus knew who He was but gave that up so He could be, "found in appearance as a man" (Philippians 2:8).

You and I are already "found in appearance as a man," so there is no surrendering of deity on our part to become humanity. In that case, let our minds think like Jesus thought; we are a representation of God on this earth!

Further into this letter to the Philippians, Paul encourages us to "think on these things" in our daily walk with God. These "things" are what are true, honest, just, pure, lovely, of good report, virtuous, and praiseworthy (Philippians 4:8). If we can train our minds to dwell on these things instead of sin-consciousness, guilt and condemnation, "the God of peace will be with you" (Philippians 4:9).

"Pastor Paul, do you mean to say that if we line up our minds to think in the manner that God thinks of us, we will automatically produce the fruit of the Spirit?"

I *do* mean to say that, but I can't take the credit for originating the thought. Peter told the recipients of his second epistle that they should be showing forth various fruits of the Spirit. He promoted a fruitful lifestyle and a full knowledge of the Lord Jesus Christ.

"But also for this very reason, giving all diligence, add to your faith virtue, to virtue knowledge, to knowledge self-control, to self-control perseverance, to perseverance godliness, to godliness brotherly kindness, and to brotherly kindness love. For if these things are yours and abound, you will be neither barren nor unfruitful in the knowledge of our Lord Jesus Christ" (2 Peter 1:5-8).

Notice that if these things are in you in abundance, you will never lack the fruitfulness that comes with knowing Jesus. But you may also notice that we are responsible for adding these things to our lives. How can this be? Is it possible Peter felt that Christians could create fruit in their lives by a certain work? The answer is found in the next verse, in which Peter explains the kind of person who lacks the fruit.

"But he that lacks these things is blind, and cannot see afar off, and has forgotten that he was purged from his old sins" (2 Peter 1:9 KJV).

If the fruit of the Spirit is not springing forth in your life, you have a form of spiritual blindness and are unable to see "far off." The Greek for "cannot see far off" is "see only what is near." This sort of blindness doesn't mean you are lost. You can only see what is on the surface, rather than what is deep.

The deeper reason the fruit isn't materializing in many lives is the last statement of that ninth verse: "and has forgotten that he was purged from his old sins." The word "forgotten" is the phrase "forgot to receive" in Greek, showing us that if we forget to receive forgiveness of sins, we can expect no fruit to spring forth.

Believer, it is time to remember what time and trials have caused far too many of us to forget: we are forgiven! When you forget this crucial aspect of your salvation, it is impossible for you to show spiritual development and maturity.

Speak What You Believe

Once your mind is in order, thinking about the things that the Father thinks about you, you are ready to produce fruit and to rest in the finished work of Jesus Christ. As you become convinced in your heart and mind of what He has made you to be, it is time to let your faith come out in the way you talk.

"And since we have the same spirit of faith, according to what is written, 'I believed and therefore I spoke,' we also believe and therefore speak" (2 Corinthians 4:13).

According to the faith that has built up in your heart as you have been reading and understanding who you are in Christ, you can now open your mouth and speak the things you believe. It is important for your talk to reflect your mind, for the words you say about who you are in Christ show how you really feel. I am not advocating that you lie and say things about your standing that you don't believe. I am trying, through the Word of God, to change how you feel about your standing so that your tongue will change right along with it!

The key to loving life and seeing good days is to learn to stop saying things that do not agree with God (1 Peter 3:10). Refrain from viewing yourself as a "sinner saved by grace," for you are no longer a sinner. Stop thinking that your sickness or disease is a test or a punishment from God because He can't tempt with evil, and Jesus has already been punished. Never again think that your righteousness is tied to your performance or that your salvation is tied to your morality. If you stop thinking it, you will stop saying it; if you stop saying it, you will love life and see good days.

Stop Blaming the Devil

The quicker you get your eyes and concentration off the devil, the better off you will be. Listen, believer, the devil is a defeated foe! Jesus came to destroy both him and his works (Hebrews 2:14; 1 John 3:8). Satan is an accuser and an adversary, but he is powerless to harm you in any way, for his weaponry has been rendered useless by the power of the blood of Jesus Christ. You are free from all his tricks, and even the curse can no longer find you (Galatians 3:13).

With that said, it is necessary to be on guard for the traps and pitfalls he might place in front of you. He is still a thief and is on the hunt. In order to do you harm, he has to use your ignorance of his defeat against you. The more you are full of the knowledge of what Christ has accomplished for you and in you, the less vulnerable you are to the wiles of the devil.

In Ephesians 4:27, Paul said not to, "give place to the devil." This shows us that we can, in fact, give Satan a position in our lives, but in order for him to have a place, we must give it to him. This is encouraging, for it means that the devil can't just run into our lives and do whatever he wants. Praise God!

The context of this verse says, "Be angry, and do not sin: do not let the sun go down on your wrath" (Ephesians 4:26). Through this, we know that anger is okay—as long as it doesn't lead to sin. How can it lead to sin? If the sun goes down on our wrath, our anger has set in without us dealing with the source of it. Thus, the seed of sin has begun. These two actions cause us to give place to the devil. Can you see how, beginning with one circumstance, a chain of events led to allowing Satan to operate in our life?

When we allow resentment, unforgiveness, or any other problem to stir inside our hearts, we are giving the enemy a place to stand in our lives. Jesus told the church that we have the power to bind and release. Whatever we bind on this earth is also bound in heaven (Matthew 16:19), which means that if we are bound by anger or jealousy, heaven is kept from moving with authority in our lives.

This in no way puts works back into our righteousness, for we are righteous whether we are bound or not! This does, however, place a responsibility on us to allow grace to work in every area of our lives if we are going to experience freedom and power. When we feed our anger or resentments (or any other lust in our flesh for that matter), we are keeping ourselves bound to that emotion, and we are binding others who are involved in our lives as well. Paul encouraged the church at Corinth to forgive a fallen brother because unforgiveness in their hearts toward another would set them up, "Lest Satan should take advantage of us; for we are not ignorant of his devices" (2 Corinthians 2:11).

You can stop blaming the devil for problems, but please be wise enough not to leave the door wide open for his temptations (Romans 13:14). For example, if you know you have had a drinking problem, it is probably not wise to spend a lot of time in places that serve alcohol. If you are trying to quit smoking, don't leave the pack of cigarettes out in plain sight. These aren't "works unto righteousness"; they are just commonsense pieces of advice.

Paul knew that the Corinthians were the temple of the Holy Spirit (just like you and me), but he still warned them to "Flee sexual immorality" (1 Corinthians 6:18). Just because you are God's righteousness and you know it and gladly proclaim it, doesn't mean that you should walk into every harmful situation. Listen carefully in your spirit, for the voice of the Holy Spirit will always lead and guide you into truth.

Don't Get in Your Own Way

We have all heard the statement, "I am my own worst enemy," but it may be most true in relation to how some Christians live! Paul instructed his young protégé Timothy to teach, "Those that oppose themselves; if God peradventure will give them repentance to the acknowledging of the truth; and that they may recover themselves out of the snare of the devil, who are taken captive by him at his will" (2 Timothy 2:25, 26 KJV).

Simply put, some believers "oppose themselves," and while this statement appears only once in Greek in the entire New Testament, it is a compound of two Greek words meaning "opposite" and "to make a covenant." Paul is warning Timothy that some believers are going to oppose the covenant that has been cut for them. There is no simpler way to do this than to condemn oneself. If you live under guilt and condemnation, you are opposing the covenant that has been cut on your behalf. Condemnation then makes you become your own worst enemy!

Paul mentions that if Timothy will instruct them with meekness, perhaps God will convince them to repent and acknowledge the truth. This is a clear-cut case of repentance being necessary in the life of a believer, as he must change his mind about who God is and what He has accomplished on his behalf. If he will acknowledge the truth, which is that God has punished all of his sins in the body of Christ and that he is reconciled to

God through the finished work, he will recover himself from the snare that the devil has laid for him. Again, God has finished the work; Satan is a defeated foe, and you have become wise enough to get out of your own way. Praise God!

"The Apostle Paul told believers at Corinth to examine their self to prove that they were in the faith. Doesn't this teach us that we should do self-examination to confirm that we are still keeping our faith in Christ?"

Paul did, in fact, tell the Corinthian believers to examine themselves. Look at both that portion of Scripture and the statement immediately following it. Notice the habit of reinforcement being used by Paul yet again.

"Examine yourselves as to whether you are in the faith. Test yourselves. Do you not know yourselves, that Jesus Christ is in you? Unless indeed you are disqualified" (2 Corinthians 13:5).

The self-examination of the saints is not to see whether they are still saved but to reinforce information they should already know. Paul uses the same "Know ye not" phrase that he made so popular in Romans (6:3, 16; 7:1) and earlier in 1 Corinthians (6:15–16, 19). He is reinforcing the knowledge that Jesus Christ is in them and encouraging them to prove it to themselves.

I can spend all day telling you that you are His righteousness through your faith in the finished work, but that knowledge will do you no good until you prove it to your own self. You must convince yourself that these words are true, because no one else has the power to make you believe what the Bible says about you. This book can't do it, your pastor can't do it, and your religious heritage can't do it. Let every man be fully persuaded in his own mind (Romans 14:5).

In the next few chapters, we dig deeper into the day-to-day walk of the believer, bringing hope and encouragement to you in your quest for His transformation. We will show you even more about true righteousness and holiness and how a thorough knowledge of who He is and what He has done will cause you to live the way you have always dreamed of living.

I believe that, together, we have already accomplished a lot. But I realize we have much farther to go! You are learning more and more about the holiness of God and how to bring it out in the different areas of your life. Peter told the church to be holy in all manner of lifestyle, and we are learning to do it the same way that he instructed: Be holy as God is holy (1 Peter 1:15, 16). How is God holy: from the outside in or from the inside out? Of course, He is holy all the way through, but our understanding of Transfiguration has taught us that it is truly from the inside out. Therefore, true holiness on our part will start on the inside and work its way out. Get ready to see even more of His glory manifest in you and out of you as we learn greater truths about His finished work!

Dealing with Sin | 11

Let's face a solid truth: we all have to deal with sin. Even though we understand the finished work of Christ, and we know that our old man has been crucified with Christ, we have to admit that failure and mistakes happen. At this point in the book, we have learned to view Christianity as a relationship rather than a religion, freeing us to live the abundant life. We have also learned that we are no longer under the law but under grace. And that grace is a person, and His name is Jesus. Due to this, we know that Satan is a defeated foe and sin is a nonissue, but we also know that we hate to fail!

Just because sin is a nonissue due to the finished work, let's not fall into the trap of believing that it is not a big deal. Remember, when a believer sins, he is committing an act that is so far below his position as to be considered embarrassing, no matter what the offense might be. These actions can bring shame to your character, your reputation, your family, and your church. Some sins even bring fracture and pain to those around us and to those who love and care for us. These consequences can last a lifetime and leave scars that never go away.

Can you see how sin has been dealt with by Jesus but can still have huge ramifications in our lives? Considering what we know about resting in the finished work and allowing the Holy Spirit to effortlessly transform us, I want to introduce you to the rest of your life: one of abundance, blessing, joy, and total freedom from the dominion of sin.

Never forget that Jesus has dealt with your sin issue, so you should give up the "just try harder" mentality and begin to trust. How you carry out your trust in His finished work will always be the major issue of your Christianity. The Holy Spirit within you will always point to Jesus, as He is the source of your victory. Conversely, the enemy will work hard at getting you to focus your attention on yourself, rather than on Jesus, pointing out your undesirable behavior, your sin, your mistakes, and your flaws. He will deny your righteousness and your forgiveness of sins. He will declare you guilty and condemned and will lead you to a life of works and effort.

Satan started his work against mankind in the Garden of Eden, first appearing in the form of a serpent. He hasn't lost that title, as Revelation 12:9 calls him "that old serpent." His first attack against Eve was to lead her to the Tree of Knowledge of Good and Evil, convincing her that there was righteousness to be had in eating its fruit, which God had denied her. From then, even until now, he has been deceiving man into believing there are works that can be done that will teach us the difference between what is good and what is evil.

Instead of living by a consciousness of good and evil or "rights and wrongs," the believer lives by the discernment of the Holy Spirit within him. Law consists of a system of rights and wrongs, but grace is full of the Spirit of discernment, where believers live according to the righteousness, peace, and joy in the Holy Ghost they sense in their heart (Romans 14:17).

Remember a truth that we have covered before: law demands righteousness from you, while grace provides His righteousness to you. Hallelujah!

Living by the discernment of the Holy Spirit is the highest form of life and is likened to eating strong meat. Every other form of living is the shallow milk that is consumed by the immature. The author of Hebrews said, "Every one that uses milk is unskillful in the word of righteousness: for he is a babe. But strong meat belongs to them that are of full age, even those who by reason of use have their senses exercised to discern both good and evil" (Hebrews 5:13, 14 KJV).

"Doesn't that verse prove that we should live by the letter of the law until we are mature in the Lord and then we can learn to live by discernment?"

Taken all by itself, those verses in Hebrews may sound very much like the author means for young converts to be governed by the law, while older saints can listen to the Spirit. But elsewhere, we learn a bit more.

To the church at Galatia, Paul addressed the Jews as children, "in bondage under the elements of the world" (Galatians 4:3), but then pointed out that when it was the appointed time, God sent His Son, "To redeem those who were under the law, that we might receive the adoption as sons"

(Galatians 4:5). The Greek word for "adoption" insinuates "fully grown sons" or "sonship," meaning that we have been brought into the family of God as fully grown sons.

Can you see that Paul calls those that live under the law children? You and I aren't little children in the eyes of our Father; we are grown sons, who have received an inheritance in Christ.

Of course, we are not fully developed in every area, because we are still ignorant in some ways and regarding many things. However, we are not babies but grown men and women, capable of living by the discernment of the Holy Spirit within our hearts rather than by our conscience. To live by "works righteousness" instead of the "word of righteousness" is to drink milk, when we should be eating meat.

Just as that serpent deceived Eve into eating from the Tree of Knowledge of Good and Evil, teaching her to live by her knowledge of what is right and wrong, Satan will still try to draw believers to that place. The Scribes and Pharisees were doing this during the time of Christ, placing more and more restrictions on people, while basking in their own self-righteousness.

John the Baptist called the Pharisees and Sadducees a, "Brood of vipers!" (Matthew 3:7). Notice the snake reference, which places the religion of self-righteousness in the same category as Satan in the Garden. John goes on to include another important piece from the Garden story, stating, "And even now the ax is laid to the root of the trees. Therefore every tree which does not bear good fruit is cut down and thrown into the fire" (Matthew 3:10).

John was a precursor of Jesus, sent to lay a path for the Messiah. He baptized men by water in anticipation of a Spirit baptism, in which Jesus would enter their hearts by faith. He preached that with Jesus, came the cutting out at the root of the very tree in which these "vipers" lived. That tree was most assuredly a metaphor for the Tree of Knowledge of Good and Evil, which had doomed man to a life of living by his conscience. The arrival of Christ guaranteed a new way to live, where the old tree would be replaced by a new tree, one forged on a hill called Calvary. Through Christ, we become fruit producers in a way that we could never have been before.

Believer, it is so important that you allow the finished work of Christ to cut the roots of the old tree from your life. This will often seem like a daily experience at the foot of Christ, not with you being re-crucified to your old nature, but with you having to learn to rest all over again, refusing to trust in your own works for righteousness.

The author of Hebrews said that "For he who has entered His rest has himself also ceased from his works as God did from His" (Hebrews 4:10).

We cannot enter into His rest as long as we depend on our own works of righteousness in any way. We must learn to rest from our labors and view His finished work as the ultimate labor.

Due to how difficult it can be to get our hands off our own victory, it is no wonder that the author goes on to say, "Let us labor therefore to enter into that rest" (Hebrews 4:11 KJV). Did you notice that entering into the rest of the Lord is going to take some labor? No, this verse does not mean that we should labor during this lifetime so that we can rest in heaven. There is no indication of this at all. Instead, it means that, due to the fact that our nature screams inside of us to do something to please or help God, the most difficult thing about Christianity will be to just rest in Jesus.

Now, do you understand why I say that sin is not the issue? The issue is learning to rest in what Jesus has accomplished. In fact, I will be as bold as to say that the single most important thing that you will do from now until the day you die is to labor to stay in His rest, even though much of the church will work hard to push you back into works.

I encourage you to feast on Scriptures that reveal Jesus as lovely and full of grace and compassion. Hear sermons that speak of the finished work and present grace radically. Read books that minister righteousness, peace, and joy in your heart, shining light on who Jesus is and what He has accomplished. As you feed on this daily, entering into His rest will become easier. All the while, you will notice the trappings of sin and failure fall away, effortlessly, as the Holy Spirit does His work.

Three Ways to Deal with Sin

By now, you have learned the right way to deal with your sins and problems daily. However, we have also learned that it is easy to slip back into works and begin trusting our efforts for victory. I want to equip you with the knowledge of how to remain at rest so that you get off of the roller coaster of Christian performance. You have become experienced enough through reading this book to identify which of these you should choose, but never forget how easy it is to get caught up in the wrong one.

1. Concentrate on it; work on defeating it; dwell on it daily; identify it wherever and whenever you can; purge it from your life; confess it constantly, even the things you don't do that you should have done; be conscious of it.

2. Ignore it and forget about it; do whatever you want, whenever you want, because it's all okay; treat it as no big deal, because only God can judge you, and you don't care what people think anyway.

3. Accept Christ as the payment for it; recognize the finished work of the cross as having removed its sting, rendering it powerless to control you; take the severity of the cross as the embodiment of God's anger against it; dwell on the loveliness of Jesus, taking light off of you and shining it brightly on Him.

As I said before, it should be obvious which one we are to do. The first one is full of law and works (and sounds very much like many churches with which we are all familiar). The second scenario assumes that anything goes. The third one is the only one that removes us from the equation and elevates Jesus. Truthfully, the first two "solutions" are all about us, while only the third is all about Jesus.

Let's give each of these three ways the proper treatment, using the Word to either combat it or support it.

If you respond to sin in the manner of our first illustration, you are constantly aware of self. This is called being "sin-conscious" and is often applauded as the thing that "good" Christians do if they take sin seriously. Actually, this sin-consciousness will lead you to self-consciousness, because the end results will always lead you to rely on your own ability to overcome sin by effort and works. In short, you are changing you by exerting the proper amount of effort and concentration on living right. There is no room for the finished work here, for God obviously needs your help.

Many will counter the previous paragraph by stating that these things are necessary to show you that Jesus is the answer. They warn that if you aren't diligent about sin, you will fall into it before you realize it. This school of thought puts heavy emphasis on sin itself, identifying it in every way possible. The messages will often point out sin in movies, television, music, and daily life; they even try to shine light on sin in creative and interesting ways. You leave these sermons with more consciousness of sin.

That sounds very holy, doesn't it? It does if you aren't aware of what happened to the Israelites under the system of sacrificial laws. Let's break down the first few verses of Hebrews 10 to find out what law did to the Jews.

"For the law, having a shadow of the good things to come, and not the very image of the things, can never with these same sacrifices which they offer continually year by year, make those who approach perfect" (Hebrews 10:1).

The law was a shadow of good things that were to come. These good things have arrived in the person of Jesus and in the Comforter, the Holy Spirit. However, the sacrificial system for sin that was instituted by the law, which demanded a blood sacrifice of a spotless animal, could never make men perfect on the inside.

"For then would they not have ceased to be offered? For the worshippers, once purified, would have had no more consciousness of sins" (Hebrews 10:2).

If they had been made clean on the inside, there would not have been a need to keep offering sacrifices. Notice the text does not say that if they had stopped sinning there would be no need for more offerings. Rather, if they had been purged of their sins, they would stop concentrating on them. The author is most certainly not praising a lifestyle of sin-consciousness but showing us that sin-consciousness is a result of thinking you are not cleansed.

"But in those sacrifices there is a reminder of sins every year" (Hebrews 10:3).

Every time the high priest offered up a sacrifice on the Day of Atonement for the sins of Israel, by the very nature of the sacrifice, there was a collective consciousness of sins. This means that there was a roller-coaster ride happening in the hearts of the people. They were happy that God had accepted their sacrifice, but they were reminded that they were going to have to do this all over again, as they thought of all of the things they might do wrong.

Thank God, Christ has now become our sacrifice! We need no more consciousness of sins, since Christ has shed His perfect blood to wash away all of our sins. Hebrews said this, just one chapter prior to our main text.

"How much more shall the blood of Christ, who through the eternal Spirit offered Himself without spot to God, cleanse your conscience from dead works to serve the living God?" (Hebrews 9:14)

You and I do not need to crowd our conscience with, "dead works to serve the living God." We can now serve God in liberty and in, "spirit and in truth" (John 4:23). Though the blood of bulls and goats couldn't remove sin (Hebrews 10:4), we have been made holy, "through the offering of the body of Jesus Christ once for all" (Hebrews 10:10).

Let's get back to our list of the three ways to deal with sin. Go back and look at number two and let's see what the Word says about that so-called "solution."

If someone were to treat sin the way our second illustration does, he would be ignoring both the seriousness of sin and the purpose of the cross. This individual would think that sin is a joke, if it even exists at all. The Bible calls anyone who makes a mockery of sin, a fool (Proverbs 14:9), and we know that he couldn't be born again from his old nature if he felt this way.

As for his treatment of the cross, he would have little opinion, since he doesn't think that sin is serious enough to merit a sacrificial death. Our chapter in Hebrews deals with this attitude as well.

"For if we sin willfully after we have received the knowledge of the truth, there no longer remains a sacrifice for sins" (Hebrews 10:26).

Directed at a Hebrew audience, this verse shows us that once you willfully go back to a sinful lifestyle after you know of the finished work of Christ, there is no other means by which you can be saved. Your works and your effort cannot do it, and to return to those would be to count the blood of the covenant, "a common thing" (Hebrews 10:29).

As you know, the only successful way to deal with sin is our third example. By doing these things, you show that you know you are powerless to stop sinning on your own but that you are also hidden with Christ in God and are dead to sin and works. You see all of your sins as having been punished in the body of Christ, and you recognize that the power to live right is in the finished work. You certainly take sin seriously; so seriously, in fact, that the finished work is honored in your life above all things, as God took it serious enough to offer up His only Son.

God prepared a body for Jesus, because He had taken no pleasure in the sacrificial system (Hebrews 10:5, 6). Into the body, He placed all of our sins (Romans 8:3; 2 Corinthians 5:21; 1 Peter 2:24), and He offered that body as a sacrifice for the sins of the world (Hebrews 10:10). Now that the same Jesus sits at the right hand of the Father (Hebrews 10:12), and through His sacrifice, He perfects everyone who accepts Him by faith (Hebrews 10:14). He also puts His Spirit into the hearts of His people to testify to the good news that "their sins and their lawless deeds will I remember no more" (Hebrews 10:17). Can you believe this? All of this good news is packed into one chapter from the book of Hebrews. Amazing!

Paul wrote to the Corinthian church about the issue of how people deal with certain aspects of the gospel. In this chapter, we have dealt with how to deal with sin, but in his first letter to Corinth, he wrote of how people were dealing with the message of radical grace and the finished work. Notice that he breaks them into three categories as well. (Where do you think we got the idea?)

> "But we preach Christ crucified, to the Jews a stumbling block and to the Greeks foolishness, but to those who are called, both Jews and Greeks, Christ the power of God and the wisdom of God" (1 Corinthians 1:23, 24).

Here we have one message (the finished work of Christ), and three responses (stumbling block, foolishness, and the power of God). Look carefully at each one, and see if it doesn't mirror the three ways to deal with sin.

1. "To the Jews a stumbling block"—The Jew trusted the keeping of the law and the sacrificial system as his righteousness. The cross represented the end to the system of Jewish ceremony, thus it was a stumbling block in the path of works. The cross proved that man was hopelessly sinful and incapable of saving himself. This requires a heart of faith to accept, with a dying out to self. A Jew who trusted works simply could not view the cross in this manner, so it was a hindrance to his walk of works.

2. "To the Greeks foolishness"—The Gentile man didn't think that there was anything wrong with himself, or he perceived the death of Christ as simply another judgment of Rome against a crazy man. To have the cross presented as more than anything but an execution was foolishness to him, since sin doesn't exist, and he doesn't think he's all that bad anyway. In other words, it's foolish to think that someone would have to die for him.

3. "To them which are called, both Jews and Greeks, Christ the power of God, and the wisdom of God"—Here, Paul removes

the barrier of Jews as being on one side and Gentiles on the other, and lumps all in one basket: those who have received Christ by faith and view the finished work in a whole different light. To those, the finished work is God showing His power over sin and His showing His wisdom in knowing how to deal with the sin issue.

Paul had to deal with all kinds of people and many varied cultures, but he believed then, as I believe now, that the answer to all of the problems of humanity was the finished work of Christ on the cross. No matter your background, I believe that you, too, are seeing the power and the necessity of what Christ has done, and how important it is that you labor to enter into that rest.

We are rapidly nearing the end of our journey together, but I feel there are a few pressing things left to be discussed. I know there are many questions forming in your head, as your heart is turned onto the message of the finished work and the radical grace of God. We are going to try to answer a few of those questions in the next few chapters and shine an even brighter light on the loveliness of Jesus.

Before we cover the individual things that I know are rising within your spirit, I want to tackle one more enormous topic, and it is one that you are going to have thrown at you time and again by those who want to "qualify" the grace about which you are so excited. Some questions you have carried for several chapters are about to be answered, and you are about to be equipped to crawl out from under the yoke of the law that is so often promoted and applauded. Most important, we are going to make sure that you never end up beneath that yoke again!

Obedience: Living from the Heart
and Not the Head | 12

"But God be thanked that though you were slaves of sin, yet you obeyed from the heart that form of doctrine to which you were delivered" (Romans 6:17).

Did you know there are two primary ways to live for God? One is from the head, and the other is from the heart. I don't mean that some people claim to follow God but only have a head-knowledge of salvation, while others follow Him from a genuine change of heart. That particular example would be the difference in a sinner and a saint. That's not what I am referring to at all.

When I mention living for God from the head versus from the heart, I am referring to two different methods of obedience in our journey with the Lord. One way is full of lists and instructions, while the other is full of communication and discernment. Living from the head constitutes an ever-increasing knowledge of do's and don'ts and rights and wrongs. Living from the heart is made up of increased knowledge as well, but it is centered on the finished work of Jesus and how much we are loved and favored.

Living for the Lord from our head is illustrated through living by the law. The law demanded perfect obedience in your performance, while demanding nothing from your heart. You could keep the law to the letter but have no compassion toward others. You could recite the Ten Commandments but not be repentant in your heart toward God. The external performance of law demanded that you *know* the law; therefore, obedience came from your head, even if your heart had nothing to do with it.

Under grace, our obedience toward the Lord lies within the bounds of our knowledge of sonship. If we view ourselves as His sons and daughters, we identify ourselves as family members with the inherent rights and privileges thereof. This knowledge may begin in the head, but there is no rote repetition of lists and commands. We do not obey a regimental doctrine. Instead, we listen to the voice of the Spirit within in our hearts, leading us into righteousness, peace, and joy.

The Apostle Paul declared that the believer was free from the law, literally using the word "delivered." Deliverance denotes that we were enslaved to the demands of the law and that someone had to purchase our freedom. That someone was Jesus, and we are no longer held in a dead state to the law.

> "But now we have been delivered from the law, having died to what we were held by, so that we should serve in the newness of the Spirit and not in the oldness of the letter" (Romans 7:6).

Paul didn't assume for a moment (and neither do I) that being free from the law meant that we would live sinful, pitiful lives. He rejoiced that the believer had been made free from basing his righteousness on whether he had done everything right. He believed that we would still serve the Lord without the trappings and demands of the law but do so out of our spirit, and not according to the, "oldness of the letter."

Can you see now why I say that you can either live for the Lord from your head or from your heart? Which method have you been practicing? Are you always finding yourself thinking in terms of what is right and wrong and worried about failure? Or are you living in the liberty Christ has given you through His perfect life and death? As we said earlier, you will find that beneath the sweet embrace of God's grace, you will live better by accident than you ever did on purpose when living beneath the law of performance and works.

Let's be frank: we all want to live right, and we want to obey the voice of the Holy Spirit. Yielding our will to the will of God is a part of who we are and what we do. Paul understood this as well, and in the verse that leads into the one that we quoted at the top of the chapter about obeying from the heart, Paul shows us there are two masters to whom we can answer. I like to call Romans 6:16, the "Tale of Two Doctrines."

The Tale of Two Doctrines

So much preaching in the church today is focused on reforming the old man. Of course, by "old man" I mean who we were before we met Christ. Through this type of preaching and teaching, Satan has no trouble keeping us focused on who we used to be instead of allowing us to see who Christ has made us to be. The source for this confusion is found in the fact that we don't believe our old man is dead; we believe he is simply covered by the blood and will stay covered if we "persevere" and "stay faithful." Never forget what Paul told Corinth: "We thus judge, that if one died for all, then were all dead" (2 Corinthians 5:14 KJV).

The old you is gone, and the new you has been created after God in righteousness and true holiness (Ephesians 4:24). With that in mind, you can now face the world, fully armed to make the right decisions about how you are going to live and conduct yourself. If you don't know that you are a son and not a slave, it is probable you will make decisions that are likened to someone beneath your standing. If you know you are a son, there is a certain sense of pride in that knowledge that makes sin and error seem beneath you.

Paul appealed to that very knowledge when he asked, "Do you not know that to whom you present yourselves slaves to obey, you are that one's slaves whom you obey, whether of sin leading to death, or of obedience leading to righteousness?" (Romans 6:16). Aside from the question Paul posed, did you notice there are two ways to conduct oneself? Let's look at each part of the sentence as two distinct forms of doctrine.

"Sin leading to death"
or
"Obedience leading to righteousness"

We can either yield our lives to one doctrine or the other. However, notice that these are forms of doctrines, *not cause and effect*. It doesn't say if I sin, that will lead to my death; nor does it say if I am obedient, that will lead to my being righteous. Instead, it introduces two indisputable facts of the spirit realm.

There are two laws at work in the spirit realm today. I know we have used the word "law" in a largely negative sense until this point, but for the purpose of this segment, I want you to see these laws as two rock-solid methods of conducting ourselves. Everyone in the world, regardless of religion or lack thereof, is living in one of these two systems.

"For the law of the Spirit of life in Christ Jesus has made me free from the law of sin and death" (Romans 8:2).

Did you notice that one law has set us free from the other law? The "Law of the Spirit of Life," which comes by knowing Jesus Christ, has made us free from the "Law of Sin and Death." This verse is a couple of chapters after our key text in Romans 6, but the idea is the same. Believers have simply moved from one doctrine to the other.

If one law has freed us from the other, the law we are in now must be greater than the one from which we were delivered. In short, the Law of the Spirit of Life trumps the Law of Sin and Death. The Spirit is stronger than the sin. Life is stronger than death. It didn't take a rocket scientist to figure that out!

Let's plug that same philosophy into Romans 6:16. The first law is "sin leading to death," and the second is "obedience leading to righteousness." The latter must be greater than the former, thus a higher form of life is found in the doctrine of obedience leading to righteousness than could ever be found in the doctrine of sin leading to death. We are told that we will live according to the one we yield to, thus the responsibility of choice falls on our shoulders.

The system of sin leading to death is the system of the world and every unbeliever. In this system, you are led by your nature to sin. Due to the fall of Adam, sin comes easily, and death is always the end result (Romans 5:12). The longer you live in sin, the easier and more habitual sin becomes, until you are a literal slave to uncleanness and one sin just leads to another (Romans 6:19).

One day you were introduced to the love of God and the sacrifice of His Son, Jesus. You were impressed with His love and loveliness, and His goodness led you to change your mind about who He was and what He was all about. You invited Jesus to be the Lord of your life and to take over where you had miserably failed. In that moment, you obeyed from the heart, and your obedience led to you instantly being made righteous in the eyes of God.

Notice I did not say that as you are obedient, you are declared righteous. As we established in previous chapters, *you are declared righteous* the moment you place faith in Jesus, *because Jesus was made to be sin for you.* Because of this, verse 16 cannot be talking about living a life of obedience to written regulations and laws in order to be declared righteous. Instead, it is talking about living under the doctrine of righteousness without the law.

The choice is ours as to under which doctrine we live. To go back and live under the doctrine of sin unto death is to choose a lifestyle of which we should be ashamed. Of this choice, Paul asked, "What fruit did you have then in the things of which you are now ashamed?" (Romans 6:21). In other words, how good was your life when you were doing the things that now seem embarrassing?

"Pastor, if living in the doctrine of sin leading to death leads sinners to a certain death, then if a believer lives under the same system, wouldn't he have hell as his destination as well?"

Remember, Jesus came to pay for the sins of humanity, and not just for those of us who believe, "but also for the whole world" (1 John 2:2). Unbelievers do not go to hell because they sin but because they reject the sacrifice of Jesus Christ (John 3:18, 19, 36). It is continuing beneath the doctrine of sin leading to death that makes a sinner what he is. If he turns in his heart to Christ, he would be obedient to the command of God, and that would make him righteous.

When a believer sins, he is not entering back into the old doctrine of sin unto death, for he has already died to sin and should consider himself dead to its dominion (Romans 6:11, 14). His sin brings shame and embarrassment, and possibly scars his reputation, but it does not place him back under his old lifestyle. That old man is dead!

For a believer to go back under the system of sin leading to death, he would have to start governing himself on his performance, considering himself righteous based on righteous acts, and have to earn all of his goodness and favor. This is how the world lives! The very system is broken, so a believer has no business living in it.

If a saint were to stay there long enough, he would begin to listen to the old habits that lie dormant in him. We all sinned so frequently that sin became habitual. If we return to the old system of the world, sin returns in like fashion, just like riding a bicycle.

However, even though a believer might go back to that form of doctrine, death is not his end, for Jesus paid for his sin through His death. In short, he lives his life on the road that leads to destruction, rather than the one that leads to life.

"But Pastor, if he is living on the road that leads to destruction, isn't he heading for hell? Jesus said that the way is straight and narrow that leads to life and few there be that find it."

Believer, there are many saints living on the road that leads to destruction, because it is so easy to live on it. That road doesn't lead to hell: it leads to destruction, which is the Greek word *apoleia*, and while it can mean "hell," it is also translated as "waste." The only way to know for sure which definition is implied is to read the context.

The next verse does indeed declare, "Because strait is the gate, and narrow is the way, which leadeth unto life, and few there be that find it" (Matthew 7:14 KJV). Notice that Jesus doesn't tell us what kind of life, unlike John 3:16, where He specifically says, "everlasting life." Without an adjective, all we know for sure is that there is a way that is narrow, a gate that is slim, and not many people are going to use it.

Millions of people, in the church and in the world, are traveling down a broad road, wasting away their lives. Some of them are believers, who are the righteousness of God in Christ but far from living like it. They are governed by their passions and lusts, and they live with the same distresses and discouragements that unbelievers bear.

There is also a remnant of believers who have chosen to live in the doctrine of "obedience leading to righteousness." Few people walk this path, because it is a pride-busting, selfless lifestyle, where Jesus is glorified as the only way, truth, and life. The souls on this path don't look to a list of instructions on how to live but listen to the sensitive sound of the Holy Spirit within their hearts. This path is full of risks, because grace is risky, freeing people from the trappings of control and religion, but it is also the only path with life, and Jesus described it as, "life more abundant" (John 10:10).

"I understand the concept of living in one of these two doctrines, but what does 'obedience leading to righteousness' mean if not, 'Obey and you will be considered righteous'?"

Friend, the power of the good news of Jesus Christ is wrapped up in the simple message that Jesus was obedient so that you could be saved and blessed. To preach that you are righteous by obedient works is to remove the glory of that powerful message. In fact, to preach that obedience brings righteousness will leave no room for the message of grace.

The obedience that Paul is talking about has already been discussed, earlier in his letter to Rome.

"For as by one man's disobedience many were made sinners, so also by one Man's obedience many will be made righteous" (Romans 5:19).

136

You are made righteous by *His* obedience. He was obedient unto death and then suffered the wrath of the Father for you and me. To live and walk in the doctrine of obedience unto righteousness is to accept that He was obedient so we can be righteous. This lifestyle is one where we rest in His finished work, realizing we are who we are only because of who He is.

Let's go back to our source Scripture one more time to learn another powerful truth about living in true obedience.

"Do you not know that to whom you present yourselves slaves to obey, you are that one's slaves whom you obey, whether of sin leading to death, or of obedience leading to righteousness?" (Romans 6:16).

Paul uses the word "obey" twice in this verse. The first time it is, "slaves to obey," and the second is, "you obey." They appear to be the same thing, but in the original Greek, in which Paul penned the words, he uses two slightly different phrases.

The first usage is the Greek word *hupakoa,* which means "to comply or obey." That makes sense, as Paul has just told the reader that whoever he yields himself over to is to whom he will comply. This definition fits our English understanding of obedience perfectly.

However, Paul's second usage of "you obey" is the Greek word *hupakuo,* which means "to listen to." Its usage shows us that whoever you yield to is who you will comply to and to whose doctrine you will begin to listen to as your source of strength.

Let's put it this way: whatever you yield to will dominate you, and you will become a servant to it, because you will listen to it the most. Simply put, what you listen to is what you feed on, and what you feed on is what you become! (Good!)

Listen to teaching and preaching that emphasizes the message of sin-consciousness, and you will always concentrate on sin. If these sermons and lessons lead you to believe that if you sin that you will die or that God will strike you with disease or illness, you will fall back under the old doctrine of performance-based Christianity. You will have no choice, for you are feeding on that kind of bread.

Listen to teaching and preaching that emphasizes the finished work of Christ and the loveliness of Jesus, and you will always concentrate on Him. This kind of doctrine will convince you that God's wrath has been exhausted in the body of Christ and that His grace flows freely into you, blessing you in spite of you, chasing you down because of the Jesus who lives in you. In this, you will find strength, hope, and victory over sin, because you are feeding on the Bread of Life!

Saint, it is not only important what you hear but how you hear it. You can hear messages on Jesus and still see Him as distant and cold, even though the same Bible used to preach the loveliness of Jesus is being used to deliver the message. Hear of Him through the lens of what He came to do and what He has done for you. Jesus warned us that how we hear is vital (Luke 8:18), so hear of your Jesus through the doctrine of obedience leading to righteousness.

I realize this can mean an absolute overhaul of some of our deeply held beliefs. It could even mean we throw out some of our Christian books and materials that have heavy emphasis on performance-based Christianity, works, effort. Sarah demanded that Hagar and Ishmael be cast out of her house, and Paul described them as, "bondage with her children," meaning that Ishmael was the by-product of law and bondage (Galatians 4:25, 30). Cast out all remnants of bondage, for you have no room for that which makes the finished work look unfinished.

Plant yourself in a place where the loveliness of Jesus is emphasized and where grace is taught in all its beauty and power. Don't be afraid to be a radical when it comes to proclaiming just how wonderful God's grace and favor have been in your life. Learn to see His favor in each and every area.

Two Doctrines = Two Kinds of Knowledge

By necessity, with two different and distinct doctrines of governing one's life come two distinct kinds of knowledge. Remember that we opened this chapter talking about living from the head versus living from the heart. Living in either of those manners will require that either your head or your heart be filled with the knowledge that is necessary to operate that way.

If you live from the heart, your heart must be full of His knowledge, which can only be achieved by His filling you up. If you live from the head, your head will be full of knowledge that can most certainly be achieved by you filling you up! This concept can be proven by using the Old Testament for the head and the New Testament for the heart.

Under the Old Covenant, God placed the written law in front of the children of Israel so they could study it and memorize it to the letter. They were given a command and told to obey it and to pass it on to future generations. Look at an example of a law given by God and followed by His commands:

"You shall love the LORD your God with all your heart, with all your soul, and with all your strength. And these words which I command you today shall be in your heart. You shall teach them diligently to your children, and shall talk of them when you sit in your house, when you walk by the way, when you lie down, and when you rise up. You shall bind them as a sign on your hand, and they shall be as frontlets between your eyes" (Deuteronomy 6:5–8).

First, I want you to notice the command is a pretty heavy one: to love God with all of your heart, soul, and strength. Can you honestly say you can do this on your own power? I know that my heart, soul, and strength sometime drift and show love in other areas. This command comes with no support system; simply a command. No righteousness is to be found here, for this is over our heads. In fact, the chapter closes with, "Then it will be righteousness for us, if we are careful to observe all these commandments before the LORD our God, as He has commanded us" (Deuteronomy 6:25). If that be the case, if we *don't* do it, we are not righteous!

Even though God told them this law should be in their hearts, there was only one way to make sure that they were consistent in their diligence: they had to write the law everywhere, so they could always see a copy of it. This insistence on visual reinforcement of the law was due to the fact that they could not change their own hearts. Thus, they needed the law to be constantly put before their eyes.

On the other hand, we have the New Testament way of living by the heart. Peter closed his last letter with an appeal to growth.

"But grow in the grace and knowledge of our Lord and Savior Jesus Christ" (2 Peter 3:18).

Just as John 1:17 connected Jesus with "grace and truth," Peter connects Jesus with "grace and knowledge." How do I grow in grace? I can't do it by repeating Scripture over and over, but I see there is knowledge that comes with my grace. That knowledge is of Jesus Christ, and the more I learn of Him and His loveliness, the more I grow in His grace. In other words, as I grow in knowledge of Jesus, I am truly living by the heart.

Due to the change of covenants, He fills our hearts with His knowledge as we see more of His loveliness. This is what God promised when He said, "This is the covenant that I will make with them after those days, says the Lord: I will put My laws into their hearts, and in their minds I will write them" (Hebrews 10:16). Did you notice that I don't put His laws into my heart and mind? He puts them there! Good (.

"What would be the harm in learning and memorizing the law? Wouldn't it simply aid the maturation process of Christians if they knew its principles?"

I will yield toward knowing anything about the law only as it relates to the blessings that accompany keeping the law. The reason I feel this way is that Jesus has redeemed us from the curse of the law by His keeping of those laws, which means I have none of the curses on me that would accompany breaking any of them. Since I am blessed in Christ, due to His being made to be the curse, I can read the promises of the law and claim them as my own.

One of my favorite passages to preach from is Deuteronomy 28, because I get to emphasize all of the good things that are mine due to the obedience of Christ. I never preach the attached curses, for Christ has paid for me to be free from all of them. What a relaxing way to live!

"But Pastor Paul, even the Apostle Paul used the Law of Moses to teach principles. Didn't he quote 'Honor thy father and thy mother'?"

Yes, in fact, Paul did quote the Fifth Commandment in his letter to the Ephesians 6:2. However, it should be noted that Paul did not quote the attached curse, brought out in Exodus 21:17, which states that if any man curse his father or mother, he should be put to death. You can't be a proper preacher of the Law of Moses if you are only going to tell people the blessings and ignore the curses, now can you?

Jesus, who preached prior to the cross, quoted the Fifth Commandment as well, but He attached the curse to those who broke it (Matthew 15:4). Why did He do this? Because He had yet to be made the curse at Calvary. After He bore the curse, you should never have to again. Thus, Paul leaves off the curse, since he is obviously not teaching the law as a blueprint for life but as an introduction to the blessings of God. Hallelujah!

Now, back to the previous question: why is it dangerous for Christians to feed themselves on the law? Let's look at a few verses, with a little commentary, as to how Paul felt about such a thing.

- "Therefore by the deeds of the law no flesh will be justified in His sight, for by the law is the knowledge of sin" (Romans 3:20). In other words, the more you know the law, the more you understand sin. Do you think understanding sin will help you overcome it?

- "Because the law brings about wrath; for where there is no law there is no transgression" (Romans 4:15). Feed on the law, and the end result is anger; remove the law, remove the transgression.

- "For until the law sin was in the world, but sin is not imputed when there is no law" (Romans 5:13). Sin exists without the law, but the advent of law is what makes sin count against man.

- "But sin, taking opportunity by the commandment, produced in me all manner of evil desire. For apart from the law sin was dead" (Romans 7:8). Sin actually uses the commandment to work in our lives. Take the law away, and sin has no legs.

- "I was alive once without the law, but when the commandment came, sin revived, and I died" (Romans 7:9). Paul was living fine without the law but then it was introduced, and the Tenth Commandment came (verse 7), causing a revival of sin, which killed his joy. Want a sin revival? Introduce the law!

- "The sting of death is sin, and the strength of sin is the law" (1 Corinthians 15:56). Death stings those who are living under sin. Sin receives its power and authority from the law.

I hope through these verses you are beginning to understand the danger of feeding on the law of works for righteousness. Though the law of God is just, holy, and good (Romans 7:12), it has no power to save me from my sinfulness. You and I have been given a new and living way, which is made possible due to Jesus' fulfilling of the law and finishing the work.

The Curse of the Law

One final thought before we move on to a very important discussion about what we are going to do with all of this grace knowledge in this final hour: you are blessed in Christ, because you have placed your faith in what Jesus has accomplished for you. Paul said this means you are, "blessed with faithful Abraham" (Galatians 3:9). Remember, Abraham received all of his blessings through no works of his own. That is why Paul wrote the next verse, and I want it to loom large in your heart and in your mind.

"For as many as are of the works of the law are under the curse; for it is written, 'Cursed is everyone who does not continue in all things which are written in the book of the law, to do them'" (Galatians 3:10).

If you didn't catch the importance, read it again very slowly, for we covered it in the opening chapter. But we need a constant refreshing of its power. Many of us who live under the demands of legalism and performance-based Christianity are under the curse of the law. We are not under the curse when we sin but when we try to base our goodness, our favor, our anointing, or our righteousness on our performance or lack thereof.

Don't feed for one more second on that which points at you instead of at Jesus. You have been saved to be free and to never again be beneath the weight and load of your own works and efforts. All problems with sin and failure are sourced in one way or another in the doctrine of sin unto death. Through the knowledge that is sinking into your heart as you read this chapter, you are now free to see your righteousness through His obedience instead of your own. Praise the Lord!

In Christ, we are better than we have been living. Isn't it time to step up and allow our walk to line up with our talk? We are His righteousness. Let's show it!

How Loved? "SO" Loved! | 13

I have saved this chapter until deep into the book, because I know what the reaction often is when someone mentions the love of God. Unbelievers tend to doubt us when we speak of His love, because we are conversely so quick to qualify it with, "But He expects …" They have grown weary of this confusing love. Believers are sometimes even worse, rejecting outright anything that speaks too glowingly of the love of God for fear that such a message will lead to apathy and sin.

What has happened to us that we are so afraid to make God appear loving and to make Jesus appear lovely? The Song of Solomon, which is a love song between Solomon and his wife and is typical of the romance between Christ and His church, says that He is, "altogether lovely" (Song of Solomon 5:16). If this verse is true, everything about our Jesus is completely lovely. Shouldn't that be celebrated?

Now that we have covered so much ground together in the course of this book, I feel confident that you are ready for a healthy dose of the knowledge of God's love. Actually, I don't think you could have made it to this point in your reading without picking up on just how much the Father loved Jesus and, thus, how much He must love you. But since the power of His love is so great, let's learn a bit more about this awesome aspect of God.

You can't divorce God's love from God's grace; without radical love, it is impossible for grace to be radical. For God to go to such lengths to extend the gift of salvation to the world through the sacrifice of His Son on the cross, the level of His love must be indescribable. Jesus said it best by using such a small word to describe such a big love.

"For God _so_ loved the world that He gave His only begotten Son, that whoever believes in Him should not perish but have everlasting life" (John 3:16).

Not only is this possibly the most quoted and most famous verse in the entire Bible, it may very well be the most important one, too! In it, we learn that God had such overwhelming love for the people of the world that He gave Jesus as a sacrifice so that all sin could be punished in _one_ man instead of in _all_ men. This love is what I call, "SO" love; love so big there is no explanation!

We should learn to feed our spirit man on the knowledge of God's love whenever possible. Since the root of all that happened for us at Calvary was the love of God, it makes sense that the more His love is proclaimed, the more the sacrifice at Calvary will become the centerpiece of our life. I believe one of the main reasons the cross of Christ is so misunderstood by many Christians is that they do not feed themselves daily on the love of the Father toward humanity. Without the knowledge of His love, the cross doesn't hold nearly the weight or significance it should.

One reason it so important to feed yourself on the love of God is never more evident than in the fact that the topic is so opposed and ridiculed. The enemy knows there is such power in the knowledge you are loved that if he can build a trench around that message and keep you from the fullness of its power, he can go to work on your insecurities and fears.

"There is no fear in love; but perfect love casts out fear, because fear involves torment" (1 John 4:18).

You and I do not have perfect love; our love is easily influenced by how people treat us or even by what mood we are in. The love that the Father has for us, however, is absolutely perfect and never changes, regardless of our circumstances. Thus, His love is "perfect love" and "casts out fear." If you are tormented by fear, it is a telling sign you are not resting in His perfect love for you.

One of the roadblocks to resting in His perfect love for us is our attempt to prove our love for Him. We have all been trained in the church world to "love God more," by well-intentioned ministers. The problem is that we don't really know how to accomplish that goal, so we go about to prove our love by service and works. Let's go one verse deeper in John's letter to find what he thought about Christian love.

"We love Him, because He first loved us" (1 John 4:19).

And let's put one other verse from earlier in the chapter with this as well.

"In this is love, not that we loved God, but that He loved us and sent His Son to be the propitiation for our sins" (1 John 4:10).

Now that we have these verses, let's feed our souls on two important pieces of information:

1. Love is defined not by what I do for God but what Jesus did for me at Calvary.

2. I only know how to love Him if I know how much He loves me.

These two concepts are the basis of the love of God: the cross shows us God's love, and the more we rest in the finished work, the more we learn how to express our love to the Father.

The Display of God's Love

Have you ever noticed the size of a storefront window? It is designed to be a display case for the goods of that particular business. Whatever the business owner wishes to promote for a particular sale will be featured prominently on models or with spotlights and neon. The display window is certainly not the entire store, but it may very well be what gets you to walk through the door.

In order for God to convey His love to all of us, He, too, designed a store window. Though the depths of His goodness and grace are inside the store, He knew He needed a way to convince us that He was good and gracious. He needed something to draw us off the sidewalk of life and into the wonders of His heart.

His display case would have to be impressive and convincing. It would need to convey in miniature everything He would want us to know. It would also need to show us a deeper need, so we would continue on through the door, confident that what we were looking for could be found inside.

The natural wonders and beauties of the world might make an impressive display, with sunsets and waterfalls, but none of them could speak to an individual on a personal level. Instead of drawing man closer to God, they would simply make God look big and man look small. Though impressive, it's not what God was going for, because it might lead men to feel a separation from, rather than an intimacy to God.

Perhaps humanity itself might do the trick. God could show man in a happy state, with friends and family that he loves nearby. He could show vacations and celebrations and laughter and joy, and maybe these things would convince mankind that God loves them, since their joy and love must have come from somewhere. However, alongside joy and laughter are heartache and pain, and maybe the very sight of loved ones would remind man of what he had lost instead of what he had gained. No, this display wouldn't work either.

Instead of these things, God went an entirely different route altogether. The Apostle Paul said it so well:

> "But God commendeth His love toward us, in that, while we were yet sinners, Christ died for us" (Romans 5:8 KJV).

The Greek word for "commendeth" is *sunestame,* and it means "to show or exhibit." God decided to show off His love, or exhibit His love through one sacrificial act: the death of Christ on the cross. His display case of goods, designed to draw us into the storehouse of His love, was the life, death, and resurrection of His Son, Jesus Christ.

By placing all of our sins into the sinless one, Jesus, God was showing off His radical love for humanity. Further, by doing this even before any of us had been born, much less sinned, He displays that His love is unconditional and all-encompassing. No other single act could express or display the might of God's love. If He would punish our yet-to-be-committed sins in the body of His Son so that we wouldn't be punished, He must love us in a way that cannot be explained!

I once heard an argument (from someone who placed no confidence in the Bible) that Jesus never said, "I love you," in any passage of Scripture. At first, this bothered me, and I searched the Scriptures in vain, trying to find a moment where Jesus looked at someone and said those three important words. Granted, He told us that the Father loved Him and us, but I had to admit that there was no indication that He said to His disciples, "I love you."

Then the Holy Spirit began to impress on my heart the reason we see no Scripture with Jesus saying this to someone. It was so that all of humanity could see God's love through a singular act. The sacrificial death of Jesus on the cross was one big, "I love you." Had Jesus said it to Peter, it wouldn't be fair to you and me, for we could always argue that they had a greater knowledge of His love than do we. By showing His love through

Calvary, both the early church and the modern church can have the same revelation and expression of God's love for all of us.

Know that You Are "The Beloved"

When Jesus was baptized in the Jordan River, the Holy Spirit descended upon Him in the form of a dove, and everyone present heard a voice from heaven saying, "This is my beloved Son, in whom I am well pleased" (Matthew 3:17). This vocal seal of approval from the Father would mark the ministry of Jesus, equipping Him to go about doing good and healing those oppressed by the devil (Acts 10:38). Everyone who heard it had to acknowledge that Jesus was, indeed, the beloved of God.

Though Matthew's version of the baptismal story relates that the voice of God spoke so that the entire crowd could hear, Luke's version gives a slightly different account.

"You are My beloved Son; in you I am well pleased" (Luke 3:22).

Notice that God speaks directly to Jesus rather than to the crowd. Do you suppose that He said it twice: once to the crowd and then once to Jesus? I don't believe that He did. I think that while the crowd was being witnessed to about the Father's love for the Son, Jesus was hearing it on a personal level at the same time.

While you are learning that God "so" loved the world, may you also personalize that love as if it is specifically for you and you alone! Though we know that He loves all men, why not internalize that love and take it as if He is saying it only to you? Jesus did this at Jordan, and you can do it as well.

The reason I am confident you are given biblical permission to personalize the love of Jesus for you is that we have an example of this happening in the Word. The Apostle John, who wrote five books of the New Testament, including the Gospel that bears his name, often referred to himself in his book as, "the disciple whom Jesus loved" (John 13:23; 20:2; 21:7, 20, 24). What gave him the right to call himself this? Isn't it a bit presumptuous to say this of yourself? Isn't John inferring that Jesus loved him more than He loved the other disciples?

These are all very good questions, but I think the answer is quite simple. When you know that Jesus loves you, you internalize that love and make it personal. You don't assume you are more loved than anyone else, but you know that you are loved, whether anyone else knows it.

You and I are shining examples of the glory of God's grace. Paul said as much to the church at Ephesus.

"To the praise of the glory of His grace, by which He made us accepted in the Beloved" (Ephesians 1:6).

Jesus is the beloved one, and we are accepted in Him. That means as He is loved, I am loved. Also, as He is accepted, I am accepted. Did you know the Greek word for "accepted" is *kharetoo*, which has as its root, *kharis* (grace)? Our acceptance has nothing to do with our goodness but with His goodness. Thus, His love for us has nothing to do with whether we deserve it but, rather, Jesus deserves it. Is Jesus deserving of the Father's love? What do you think?

The only other time that "kharetoo" appears in the New Testament is when the angel Gabriel appears to Mary, mother of Jesus. He tells her that she is, "highly favored" (Luke 1:28), or in Greek, she is "kharetoo." Paul uses that same word to describe the believer who is in Christ. In Jesus, we are, "highly favored," because He is beloved. Awesome!

One more thought before we move deeper into what His love provides. Do you know what the word "David" means in Hebrew? It means "beloved." David spoke Hebrew, so it was common knowledge what his name meant. The knowledge he was so beloved was what kept him from fearing the lion and the bear. Knowledge of being beloved also placed him in front of the giant Goliath, where he refused to back down in the face of danger. Only those who know they are beloved will ever bring down the giants of adversity and condemnation.

"Pastor, it's good for people to know that God loves them, but that knowledge won't help them make the right decisions when faced with temptation. They need to know God's standards!"

I readily agree that we need to know God's standards, but I also believe these have been written on our hearts by the Holy Spirit, and He is in us to remind us of them, along with the fact that all of our sins and iniquities will be remembered no more (Hebrews 10:16–17). However, where I disagree with that statement is that the knowledge of God's love won't equip people to deal with temptation. Not only do I disagree, the Word of God does, too!

Jesus went straight from Jordan to the wilderness, "to be tempted of the devil" (Matthew 4:1). In that hour of temptation, Satan threw several tricks at Christ, only to be thwarted each time. Have you ever noticed one of the things the devil did in the wilderness was question Jesus' knowledge of sonship? He says, "If You are the Son of God, command that these stones become bread" (Matthew 4:3). He was obviously listening when God declared, "This is my beloved Son," but now he wants to quiz Christ's authority as the Son.

If you have noticed the devil's attack on sonship, you have probably also noticed what Satan left out in his attack of Jesus. He *doesn't* say, "If you are the beloved Son of God," for that would remind Jesus of how loved He is. Instead, he leaves that bit about being beloved out altogether. Fortunately, Jesus never doubted His Father's love for Him and easily overcomes the temptation of the devil.

If Satan was quick to drop the "beloved" when tempting Jesus, don't you think he will try to hide the same information from you? Believer, you are dangerous to darkness when you know you are loved!

Another shining example of a son who knows he is loved is found in the Old Testament story of Joseph. The Scripture is very clear as to how his father, Israel, felt about him.

"Now Israel loved Joseph more than all his children, because he was the son of his old age: and he made him a coat of many colors" (Genesis 37:3 KJV).

The Hebrew reference for "colors" denotes a long tunic that stretches to the hands and the feet, meaning that this robe covered his entire body. Only those of aristocracy or royalty wore garments that covered their arms, for the day laborer had his arms exposed for easy movement. Can you imagine the message this sent to Joseph's brothers? By giving Joseph this coat, Jacob was declaring such a love for him that he was freeing him from all labor and effort. I'm sure that went over great!

Isaiah tells us that our Father has clothed us in a similar garment due to His love for us: "I will greatly rejoice in the LORD, my soul shall be joyful in my God; for He has clothed me with the garments of salvation, He has covered me with the robe of righteousness, as a bridegroom decks himself with ornaments, and as a bride adorns herself with her jewels" (Isaiah 61:10).

The Father adorned the prodigal in a robe, identifying him as His own in Luke 15. We have His robe of righteousness on us as a sign and seal that we are loved, with no works of righteousness ever required in order for us to maintain it.

Joseph had his coat stripped from him by his brothers, but the knowledge of his father's love was something they couldn't take away. I think this knowledge followed him everywhere he went, causing him to live above his station no matter how bad things became. If he was in prison, he served the prisoners. When he was promoted, he performed with honor. Everything he touched prospered, and Joseph never forgot who he was or from where he came.

As you know, one day his boss' wife cornered him and tried to seduce him. Joseph flatly refused her advances, stating, "How can I do this great wickedness, and sin against God?" (Genesis 39:9). I want to remind you that we are more than four hundred years from the giving of the law, so the Seventh Commandment, "Thou shalt not commit adultery," doesn't even exist yet. Without the knowledge of the law, what would keep Joseph pure? By modern ministry standards, Joseph has no chance. He has no knowledge of the written law, thus, he should fail by default.

"How can I?" does not imply that Joseph could not sin, nor that sin would be impossible for him. Rather, it shows us that he had such knowledge of sonship as to consider sin impossible. In other words, he could sin, but it would go against who he knew he was. This is a higher form of living: this is living on the knowledge of love!

As I write these words, I am so overwhelmed with the mighty love of the Father for us that it reminds me of a verse I long ago wrote the word "WOW!" next to in my Bible:

> "Behold what manner of love the Father has bestowed on us, that we should be called children of God! Therefore the world does not know us, because it did not know Him" (1 John 3:1).

No Separation

We discussed in an earlier chapter how the Apostle Paul reveals to us the gift of no condemnation in the first verse of Romans chapter 8. What we did not talk about then is very necessary to bring up now. While Romans 8 opens with, "no condemnation," it closes with, "no separation." Between them is the working of the Holy Spirit within our lives. With only one mention of the Holy Spirit prior to the eighth chapter (5:5), the text suddenly explodes with His activity, mentioning the Holy Spirit nineteen times in this chapter alone! Only when the believer rests in the gift of no condemnation, because of the finished work of Christ, does he allow the

Holy Spirit to do His perfect work in his life. The end result of the work of the Spirit will be complete knowledge of just how loved he is.

So secure is the believer in the love Christ has for him, Paul uses as many terrible circumstances he can fathom to show there is nothing that trumps God's love.

> "Who shall separate us from the love of Christ? Shall tribulation, or distress, or persecution, or famine, or nakedness, or peril, or sword?" (Romans 8:35).

Paul points out some powerful truths about God's love in these passages, beginning with our position in Christ as, "more than conquerors through Him who loved us" (Romans 8:37). The word "conquerors" in Greek speaks of, "gaining a surpassing victory," meaning that, in Christ, our victory over sin, the flesh, and the devil is an overwhelming one. We are so victorious because of what Jesus did for us, but until we grasp a singular point of that thirty-seventh verse, we do not know exactly *how* victorious we really are. Notice we are more than conquerors, "through Him who loved us." If you know how loved you are, you reap the benefits of Jesus' victory at the cross!

> "For I am persuaded that neither death nor life, nor angels nor principalities nor powers, nor things present nor things to come, nor height nor depth, nor any other created thing, shall be able to separate us from the love of God which is in Christ Jesus our Lord" (Romans 8:38, 39).

Paul's "persuasion" of verse 38 is "confident" in Greek, denoting he had become intimate enough with the Lord and His love that he could say unequivocally there was nothing in the universe that could cause God to stop loving His creation. Even, "things to come," were covered! There is no amount of technology or inventions yet thought of that could outdo or outlast the love of God. How sweet it is to know that no matter how sophisticated man becomes, or how many new ways he invents to sin against God, there is no separating man from God's abundant love and grace.

The word "separate" is particularly interesting, because it literally means "to divorce." God views His relationship with His children as both Father to son/daughter and Husband to wife. There is nothing that can ever divorce the love of God from His bride. Jesus has married Himself to us through the blood covenant of the cross. He even gave His mother away at Calvary, so He could be free to cleave to His wife (the church). What an awesome God!

Please note that the love of God is, "in Christ Jesus our Lord." Everything that God does for us is because of the finished work of Jesus Christ on the cross. We are blessed, favored, and loved, because Jesus paved the way through His sacrificial death. See your condemnation in Him, so you will never see a separation of His love from you.

Paul's Ultimate Prayer

"For this reason I bow my knees to the Father of our Lord Jesus Christ" (Ephesians 3:14).

There are various situations and circumstances that drive me to prayer. We all have them: moments where we instantly say a prayer. Whether it is the pain of someone dear to us losing a loved one or a sickness in our own family, these things cause us to say a prayer of strength and support. Of course, we also have other issues in our lives—financial, domestic, and so on—that make us bow our heads.

Paul gives us the statement, "For this reason I bow my knees," meaning that of all the reasons he might pray for his beloved church at Ephesus, this one cause is the most important. Learning of Paul's cause in praying for these saints of old should shed some light on what Paul felt all believers needed to both know and possess.

There are three principal things in Paul's prayer that he desires for each believer. Let's look at the three, with heavy emphasis on the final one, for that's the one Paul placed the most emphasis on as well.

1. "That He would grant you, according to the riches of His glory, to be strengthened with might through His Spirit in the inner man" (Ephesians 3:16).

2. "That Christ may dwell in your hearts through faith" (Ephesians 3:17).

3. "That you, being rooted and grounded in love, may be able to comprehend with all the saints what is the width and length and depth and height and to know the love of Christ which passes knowledge; that you may be filled with all the fullness of God" (Ephesians 3:17–19).

Paul's first desire is for all believers to be granted the strength that comes only through the power of the Holy Spirit. His second desire is very similar, wishing that Christ dwell in their hearts according to their faith. Notice that both of these prayers are actually already a done deal. Every believer is strengthened in his inner man only by the presence of the Holy Spirit, and he isn't even a believer if Christ doesn't dwell in his heart by faith. Paul isn't praying for a future action but praying for awareness in the believer's hearts as to what is already there.

That leads us to Paul's very detailed third request. He desires for us to be rooted and grounded not in our denomination, doctrine, works, or efforts but, "in love." Now, lest we think he is inferring we be defined by how much we love others, he goes on to establish that our comprehension includes the four directions of God's love for us: how high, how low, how deep, and how wide.

Just as the cross goes in four directions: head, feet, and each hand, the love of Christ for us covers us in every possible direction. Paul wants each of us to understand this, stating that when we begin to comprehend this, it passes all other knowledge and thereby fills us up with the fullness of God. Who doesn't want to be filled with God's fullness?

I must ask why is this not being preached over and often? Why is it becoming so difficult to hear sermons and lessons on the love of God, without a steady stream of clarification and qualification? If Paul's heartfelt desire was that believers comprehend just how bountiful and limitless the love of Christ was for them, why are we so slow to reveal that same love and loveliness?

The message of radical grace has so changed my life and ministry that I want the whole world to know that which passes all other knowledge: the love that Christ has for them! I have ceased to worry that knowledge of amazing love will lead people to apathy and failure, because I know it has caused the opposite to happen in me. Every day I come into the knowledge of His love for me, I find a deeper desire to live out His love, which has filled up my heart. The last thing I want to do is betray that love.

Believer, may we drop the fear and concern that showing people His love will cause them to take advantage of both the Father and His church? Jesus never backed away from someone, because He was afraid that if He gave too much, that individual would take advantage of Him! Trust the Lord to do this better than you can.

"How will telling a sinner that God loves him lead him to salvation? Shouldn't he be told about hell and the judgment of God so that he knows that he is lost first?"

If you meet someone who has never accepted Christ and refuses to acknowledge that he needs Him, you are meeting someone John said is deceiving himself, and the truth is not in him (1 John 1:8). This individual must come to the knowledge that he is a sinner by confessing it and then righteousness is his for free (verse 9).

However, that is an extreme case, which is why it appears only once in John's letter (Paul never dealt with it; neither did Peter). In most cases, unbelievers readily admit they have mistakes and sins in their lives, though they are often just as quick to point out how they are trying very hard or doing good things to overcome the bad. They are works driven and bound to the law, for they are convinced that their deeds will get them to heaven.

These individuals must hear how much God loves them. That love must be shown to them through the only means God gave for man to comprehend His love: the finished work of the cross. Show the sinner that God was so angry at his sin that He punished all of it in the body of His perfect Son and that Jesus is now raised from the dead so He can take up residence in his heart and give him His abundant life.

Paul believed that gospel ministry should be preached this way, and only this way, stating the goodness of God leads men to repentance (Romans 2:4). The more favor and grace that God shows toward mankind, the more man changes His mind about who God is. Since repentance is the changing of one's mind, the more men see God as loving, the more he repents.

When Jesus blessed Peter with a net-breaking load of fish, Peter fell down at His feet and cried, "Depart from me, for I am a sinful man, O Lord!" (Luke 5:8). The love and goodness of Jesus toward a man who was not living morally in any way did not cause that man to run out and take advantage of righteousness. Instead, the goodness of God to an undeserving fisherman caused that man to see his own shortcomings and to fall at the feet of Jesus. Jesus quoted none of the Ten Commandments, nor did he point out any of Peter's faults. His goodness worked then, and it will work now!

One final thought is necessary to close out this chapter on God's love. Peter had another encounter with Jesus at the end of Christ's earthly ministry. Just days after the resurrection, Peter determined that he was done fishing for men and decided to go back to fishing the old-fashioned way. The Greek for his statement, "I am going fishing" (John 21:3) is, "the final departure of one who ceases to be another's companion." Peter has failed, so he decides that he is finished.

After fishing all night and catching nothing, a familiar figure appears on the shore and calls out to Peter and his companions in the boat, ordering them to cast their nets on the right side of the ship. When their nets were filled with fish, "That disciple whom Jesus loved saith to Peter, 'It is the Lord!'" (John 21:7). We know that the disciple Jesus loved was John, but did you notice that a recognition of how loved you are gives you a special insight into identifying who Jesus is? Know He loves you, and you learn to expect a net full of fish! In other words, you see blessings too good to be true, and you say, "It is the Lord."

I was studying this passage once and began to question the Lord why Peter's nets broke the first time Jesus blessed him, but not this time in John 21:11. It seemed to me that if the nets were breaking, there were obviously more fish than if they were not breaking. It didn't make sense that Peter's first blessing should exceed his second.

Then the Spirit revealed to me an awesome truth that I want to share with you in closing. Peter's first blessing of fish was given to him in an unredeemed state, while his second was in a redeemed state. Unbelievers are blessed by God all of the time, but they have no capacity to maintain the blessings because they do not comprehend, "It is the Lord." So their nets break. Recognition that it is the Lord comes first to those who realize that they are loved. Their nets never break, though they are so full that "they were not able to draw it in because of the multitude of fish" (John 21:6). Is it better to have so much that your nets break or to have such solid nets that there are more fish than you can handle? This is the love and grace of our awesome God!

How loved are you? "SO" loved!

Loose Him, and Let Him Go! | 14

As you near the end of this book, my prayer for you is that you are beginning to see how much God loves you and that Jesus is lovely. As the revelation of His marvelous grace and favor becomes real in your heart, you will see the chains of religion and works begin to fall away. The transformation from who you were into whom He wants you to be will be less and less about you and more and more about Him. His finished work is becoming paramount in your life, and your life is no doubt changing for the better.

One of the tell-tale signs that His love is at work in you will be what you do with that love as it relates to others. It is a wonderful thing to bask in the Father's love for us, but what are we doing with that love on a daily basis in the lives of those around us?

A scribe once approached Jesus and asked Him which of the commandments was greatest in the law. Scribes were students of Jewish law, claiming to be experts in every way concerning God's commandments. This question was asked in an attempt to corner Jesus and get Him to place more emphasis on one act of morality over the other.

> "Jesus said to him, 'You shall love the LORD your God with all your heart, with all your soul, and with all your mind.' This is the first and great commandment. And the second is like it: 'You shall love your neighbor as yourself.' On these two commandments hang all the Law and the Prophets" (Matthew 22:37–40).

Jesus is describing the "greatest commandment," but He is being specific in relation to the man's question. Remember, the scribe asked which commandment was the greatest, "in the law" (Matthew 22:36).

Jesus is bringing glory back to the highest command of the law, which is for man to love God with everything that he possesses.

Of course, if we are all perfectly honest, we see how impossible it is for man to love God with his whole heart. Even when we think we love Him as much as we can, we find that we still drift in our focus or our attention toward Him or His work. In fact, have you noticed that the more you dwell on showing God how much you love Him, the more you seem to fall short? This is because Jesus is describing love under the law, a standard we are incapable of living up to.

When left to describe love on His own terms, without limiting it to the law, Jesus gives us a different commandment.

"'A new commandment I give to you, that you love one another; as I have loved you, that you also love one another'" (John 13:34).

Christ commands, in no uncertain terms, that we love one another. He tells us how we are to do that: "'As I have loved you.'" Our love for one another should mirror the love He has for us. Just to make sure we understand what that love is, He repeats the command two chapters later and then adds this:

"'Greater love has no one than this, than to lay down one's life for his friends'" (John 15:13).

If you want to measure the fullness of His love, look at the fact that He laid down His life for you. To have a full revelation of His finished work is to have a full revelation of His love. Only when you have that will you be able to love other people in the right way. While the law demands that you love God, grace affords you the ability to receive God's love and give it away freely to everyone around you. Praise God!

How to Display His Love

We know that God put His love for all of mankind on display at Calvary, punishing all of our sins in the body of His Son. But how do we put His love on display in our lives? What is the most practical way to show others just how much the Father loves them?

When I first began to experience the revelation of grace in my life, it was so overwhelming that I considered just sitting on it for as long as possible. Already fully involved in active ministry, I figured to preach and teach this newfound message of radical grace would involve an overhaul in everything that I knew about the Word of God. Believe me, it was tempting to just rest in the freedom and keep it all to myself!

The problem with sitting on this wonderful message is that it burns inside and demands a release. Just like Jeremiah, sitting in prison and determined to never preach again, the Word will become like a fire, shut up in our bones (Jeremiah 20:9). When this happens, we realize that what we have discovered is too great to keep to ourselves. With no mandate to evangelize, and no threat hanging over our head if we don't witness to others, we find ourselves creating excuses to let people know about the goodness of God. A life of evangelism starts coming easily when we have been saturated by His grace.

Now that you are actually seeing effortless transformation in your life, get ready for the next step in the operation of grace. It's time to let Jesus go to work all around us and for us to be used in His work.

Stone Throwers vs. Stone Rollers

God originally wrote the law on two tablets of stone and gave them to Moses at the top of Mt. Sinai. Paul said these laws were, "the ministry of death, written and engraved on stones" (2 Corinthians 3:7). Seeing "death" and "engraved on stones" in the same sentence is crucial in learning how we should interpret the appearance of stones in the New Testament. If the original law was the minister of death, and it was written on stones, whenever we see stones in relation to death, we are seeing a type and shadow of the law.

I don't want to insinuate that stones or rocks are always representative of the law, for Jesus Himself is referred to as, "the stone which the builders rejected" (Acts 4:11), and the Rock in the wilderness (1 Corinthians 10:4). We also know that David brought down Goliath with a stone, thrown from a slingshot, and that rock certainly doesn't represent using the law to defeat the giant. (By the way, the stone didn't actually kill Goliath; it just knocked him down. David actually killed Goliath using the giant's own sword.)

The Gospel of John records two incidents in which stones play a huge role in the story, and both are in relation to death. These give us New Testament analogies of how the law is to be treated by the believer. The first is found in John 8, in the story of the woman caught in the act of adultery. The scribes and Pharisees bring the woman to Jesus to see how He will respond to her crime. If Jesus says she should be let go, they will accuse Him of failing to uphold Mosaic Law. If He says to stone her, they will paint Him as harsh and uncaring. Of course, Jesus will not fall into their trap.

"'He who is without sin among you, let him throw a stone at her first'" (John 8:7).

You know how this story ends, but have you ever considered what the scribes and Pharisees were attempting to cast at this woman? They were certainly going to use actual stones in the event that they actually executed her, but these stones come to represent something much larger. These represent the accusation and condemnation associated with our breaking God's law. When their hearts were laid open for God to see, the scribes and Pharisees knew that they were just as guilty as this woman, and they were forced to turn away. They were hung on their own gallows.

Fast-forward three chapters, and we find Jesus arriving in the village of Bethany, four days after the death of His friend Lazarus. Mary and Martha both believe that Lazarus will live again in the resurrection, but Jesus asserts Himself as the resurrection, promising life (John 11:25). After being led to the tomb, Jesus tells the family, "Take away the stone" (11:39), to which He is met with opposition on the part of the family. They fear that the body has begun to rot and stink, and they can't stand the thought of removing the covering.

Notice that Jesus instructs the family to take away the stone, though it is obviously not a problem for Him to remove it supernaturally. Anyone who can walk on water can roll away stones, but Jesus wants to lay the responsibility of stone removal at the feet of someone else. The command to that family is, therefore, a command to the church family today. Roll away the stone! Good Sermon!

If stones that are connected to death are representative of the law, the stone that holds back Lazarus is also representative of those things that bind and condemn us. None of us are able to uphold the strict demands of the law for our righteousness, and the longer we try, the more, "in the tomb," we remain. Yes, we are alive in Christ, but we aren't living free.

What good does it do to rise from the dead only to be trapped in your tomb forever? I have heard that several centuries ago, before dead bodies were embalmed, it was not uncommon for people to bury their loved ones with a string attached to the deceased's finger. The string ran to the surface and was attached to a little bell. This way, if the person wasn't actually dead, he could ring the bell, and someone would dig him out. When I heard this as a boy, I could only think one thing: *What if the string broke?*

Thank God, we don't exchange the tomb of sin for the tomb of Christianity! He whom the Son has set free, is free indeed (John 8:36). You have been called forth from darkness into the light, and you need not be trapped behind the demands of the law for righteousness any longer.

This book has been designed to help roll away the stone from your life, so you can live free in Jesus. It came about as a result of a decision I had to make in my life and ministry (and, thank God, due to His marvelous grace, it has been an easy one): will I be a stone thrower or a stone roller? Will I use the law to hurl guilt and condemnation at people, all the while knowing that I cannot live according to its righteous demands? Or will I roll the stone of "performance-based Christianity" out of people's way and show them the freedom that comes in Jesus? I have to answer that question, and so do you.

This job doesn't belong to pastors and ministers alone; it is the job of every believer who has experienced our Father's radical grace and favor. What we do with His grace as it relates to our lives is one thing, but what we do with this knowledge in helping others is something of equal importance.

Beloved, never be confrontational with this message of grace, for it is too pure and beautiful to be tainted by our emotions and arguments. When someone opens his heart to hear of His goodness, pour it in. But if he clings to law and works and wishes to argue, let him go. Arguments convince no one, and they lead to strife and frustration.

One more piece of advice as it regards sharing the gospel with unbelievers and radical grace with believers: never close your argument with, "I'll be praying for you." It is a condescending, patronizing thing to say and makes it appear as if you know it all and they know nothing. Perhaps they should be praying for you! Please remember what the Apostle Paul said regarding the knowledge of how free you are in grace: "Knowledge puffs up, but love edifies" (1 Corinthians 8:1). And then, "If anyone thinks that he knows anything, he knows nothing yet as he ought to know" (8:2).

"Loose Him, and Let Him Go"

After Lazarus came out of the grave, Jesus gave another command to those standing nearby: "'Loose him, and let him go'" (John 11:44). Lazarus was covered in grave clothes, which were long strips of fabric wrapped tightly around his body. Their presence kept him immobile, unable to walk properly or to use his arms. As long as these remained on him, he couldn't fully enjoy the life that he had just been granted.

Again, Jesus could have brought Lazarus out of the grave without any grave clothes on at all. After all, He Himself will come out of the tomb on Resurrection Morning without any of these rags hanging on. However, He gives the church something else to consider in its dealings with new converts.

Instead of adding works righteousness to the new convert, which seems to be our first instinct in the church, Jesus is telling us to loose them from the righteousness of self. We know this because of what these death rags represent.

"But we are all like an unclean thing, and all our righteousnesses are like filthy rags; we all fade as a leaf, and our iniquities, like the wind, have taken us away" (Isaiah 64:6).

Isaiah makes it very clear: it is not our sins that are considered filthy rags, for we don't clothe ourselves in sin. It is our attempts at righteousness and goodness that are filthy, for we wear these as protection. Adam did as much in the Garden, when he clothed himself with fig leaves, attempting to cover his wrongdoings.

Have you noticed that many people try to balance their wrongs with a list of rights? They justify their lying or cheating by saying they don't do it as much as their neighbor or that at least they don't commit adultery or steal. This is comparative righteousness and yet another form of self-justification. Paul reminded us, "Therefore by the deeds of the law no flesh will be justified in His sight, for by the law is the knowledge of sin" (Romans 3:20).

The more we point people to the righteousness that is found in Christ, the less they will focus on their own deeds for righteousness. This provides freedom, one day at a time, as the grave clothes are removed. We remove the rags steadily and methodically by showing them God's loving grace, allowing for slow movement in their walk as they grow into this knowledge. Don't expect an automatic depth of knowledge on their part, for they are just now learning to use some of the limbs that self-righteousness has held back.

Jesus told us this in His Sermon on the Mount, when He instructed His listeners on how to live in rest from day to day. He told them not to worry about what they would eat or drink or what clothes they would wear, since these were things that unbelievers worried about, and the Father had it under control. Instead of worrying, He exhorted them to seek.

"But seek first the kingdom of God and His righteousness, and all these things shall be added to you" (Matthew 6:33).

Jesus just gave us the formula for having all of the things the world desires: seek the kingdom of God and His true righteousness. His righteousness is found in the sacrifice of Jesus, where Christ was made sin so that you and I could be righteous. Dwell on *that,* and you see all things added to you. Dwell on *your* righteousness, and you will notice that the enemy keeps stealing, killing, and destroying. Which do you want?

Can you see the awesome responsibility that is held by every believer? We have been so transformed by His grace, and now we are fully equipped to share it with every open heart that will hear. Be swift to listen for those who are crying out for grace and slow to speak; be careful to season your words with His grace and His compassion. His precious sheep are too valuable to treat lightly.

Giving Voice to the Next Generation

I wish I had heard the message of radical grace when I was just a boy. There is no telling how different things might have been for me. Truthfully, I have no regrets, for I know that everything I went through to get where I am has had a huge influence on who I am and what I know. God used it all to create something beautiful, and I am grateful for that.

With that said, I intend to raise my children under the message of radical grace and to give voice to the needs, hopes, and dreams of their generation. What better way to grow up than with the knowledge that God is not mad and that the death of Jesus has satisfied His demands?

The next generation has always held a place of importance in the heart of God. With His foreknowledge, He has always known what they would face and how difficult their lives would be. This is why Jesus was so quick to embrace the children during His ministry, knowing that His love and compassion for them in childhood would have an enormous effect on their adulthood.

This attitude was evident in the Old Testament, when the prophet Jonah was told to go to Nineveh to preach repentance to that heathen nation. Jonah has been called "the Reluctant Prophet," because he was slow to heed the call of God. We know the story of his running away and then being tossed overboard, swallowed by a whale, and vomited up on the shores of Nineveh three days later.

What is often left out in the retelling of Jonah is how the book ends. Jonah had been reluctant to go to Nineveh, who were constant oppressors of Israel, and Jonah wanted God to judge and destroy them. If they were offered forgiveness, Jonah was afraid that they would accept, and God would hold back His indignation. Can you imagine a prophet being reluctant to preach, because he was afraid that the people would accept?

His worst fears came to pass, as the people of Nineveh accepted his message and repented. God spared them from his fiery judgment, and all should end happily ever after. However, the final chapter tells us that this, "displeased Jonah exceedingly, and he became angry" (Jonah 4:1), prompting him to storm out of the city and sit in the shade.

Over the course of the next couple of days, God raises a tree to offer Jonah shade and shelter. Then, He prepares a worm to destroy that tree. Following the destructive worm, God stirs up a storm, which beats upon Jonah, and causes him to be so depressed that he considers suicide (Jonah 4:8). God's object lesson has come to completion, and in the final two verses of the book, we are about to learn something remarkable about the heart of God.

"But the LORD said, 'You have had pity on the plant for which you have not labored, nor made it grow, which came up in a night and perished in a night. And should I not pity Nineveh, that great city, in which are more than 120,000 persons who cannot discern between their right hand and their left - and much livestock?'" (Jonah 4:10, 11).

Jonah is angry over the destruction of the tree, even though he did nothing to make it grow in the first place. God uses Jonah's emotion to illustrate how He feels about a city He did create, where one hundred twenty thousand people live who can't tell the difference between their right hand and their left hand. Have you ever considered what kind of people this might be? I remember teaching my kids when they were small the difference between right and left. They didn't know, but it had to be taught. God is defending Nineveh for the children's sake!

He has always had a heart for the next generation, even if that generation is raised in a heathen society. Actually, where this is the case, His grace is even more profound.

"But where sin abounded, grace abounded much more" (Romans 5:20).

What We Don't Know Will Hurt Them!

We have all heard the saying, "What you don't know will hurt you," but I think we should consider that what we don't know about covenant will not only hurt us, it will hurt the next generation. We hold the power to set free subsequent generations by rolling away their stone and removing their grave clothes. With that great power comes the possibility for tragedy, where we actually stunt the growth of our next generation by giving them an unhealthy fear of God.

A prime example of the wounding of the next generation is found in the story of Mephibosheth. We learn both who he was and what happened to him in one verse:

"Jonathan, Saul's son, had a son who was lame in his feet. He was five years old when the news about Saul and Jonathan came from Jezreel; and his nurse took him up and fled. And it happened, as she made haste to flee, that he fell and became lame. His name was Mephibosheth" (2 Samuel 4:4).

The news that prompted this disaster was that the army of Israel, including King Saul and Prince Jonathan, had been destroyed. The nurse who took care of Jonathan's son became frightened at the prospect of Saul's enemies taking the capital city, so she scooped up the child and fled. In her haste, she apparently either fell on the child or dropped him, doing permanent damage to his feet and impairing his ability to walk properly.

There are several important elements to this story that only appear in shadow on first glance. However, when viewed through the lens of the finished work, we see substance take shape.

1. David and Jonathan made a covenant in which David promised never to cut off his kindness from the house of Jonathan, meaning that David was forced by a blood oath to care for Jonathan's family (1 Samuel 20:15).

2. Saul (Jonathan's father) swore to kill David on sight out of jealous rage. David was already anointed the next king by the prophet Samuel, thus there was a national schism over who should be the rightful heir to Saul's throne. With Saul and Jonathan dead, everyone assumed that David would be vengeful and aggressive.

Before we go further, let's deal with these two points. They are very important to our topic of influence over the walk of the next generation. Can you see how a lack of knowledge about the covenant between David and Jonathan had an adverse effect on the maid's reaction? Had she known how close David and Jonathan were, she would not have panicked. She could have relaxed and been at ease, knowing that David would never do anything to harm the child since he was bound by covenant.

What she didn't know hurt Mephibosheth. She dropped the child and wounded his legs, ruining the way he walked forever. All of us want to "walk right" before the Lord, but we are often hampered by preaching and teaching that excludes the New Covenant of God's grace and peace. When the next generation hears the sounds of Old Covenant theology, it doesn't matter how much we try and mix in the New Covenant of grace. It will still destroy their walk, causing them to be lame in running this race.

What difference could have been made if the right person had known about the covenant! Equally, what difference can now be made if pastors, teachers, church-builders, and parents know about the New Covenant cut between the Father and the Son. We might spare another generation from stumbling in performance-based Christianity when it should be running in the liberty of God's grace.

3. The child is five years old when he is wounded in his legs.

4. "His name was Mephibosheth" (2 Samuel 4:4).

Hebrew numerology teaches us that five is the number of grace, and it is no coincidence that the child is five years old when this tragedy occurs, meaning, that at the very moment when grace saves us and our development begins, what we hear about God makes a profound difference on how we live.

At conversion, we are brought into the family of God by placing our faith in the finished work of Jesus Christ, and His grace saves us. It is grace that saves us and then it is grace that keeps us. *We are defined by grace.* Everything we have is a free gift of God, given to us for Christ's sake. To inject a negative view of God into someone at that moment when grace goes to work is to stunt his walk and cause him a lifetime of problems.

The name "Mephibosheth" is important here, for it comes at the end of the story rather than the beginning. This tells us that the events of the story have had a lasting effect on the boy. His birth name was not Mephibosheth, but rather Merib-baal (1 Chronicles 8:34), which means, "to contend against Baal." Baal is a generic name for false gods, so the heritage of this young man was to be one that stood against falsehood and error. What an honorable name and calling!

However, when the maid hurried from the house, ignorant of the covenant of peace between David and Jonathan, it is Merib-baal who pays the price, having his legs permanently ruined. His name is changed to Mephibosheth, which is a combination of two Hebrew words meaning "separate" and "shame." When God is made to appear angry and vengeful, men feel separated from His presence and are constantly ashamed.

"And hope makes not ashamed; because the love of God is shed abroad in our hearts by the Holy Ghost which is given unto us" (Romans 5:5 KJV).

Christ is our hope and our salvation, so we should never be ashamed again!

Several years later, David remembers the covenant he cut with Jonathan and inquires as to whether there is anyone left from the house of Jonathan so that he may show kindness to him, "for Jonathan's sake" (2 Samuel 9:1). In this instance, David is a type of God, who always deals with the earth through the covenant by which He is bound. He cut covenant with His Son at Calvary and now deals with humanity through the lens of the cross. Jonathan is a type of the smitten Savior, and whatever God does for you and me, He does it for Jesus' sake.

"And be ye kind one to another, tenderhearted, forgiving one another, even as God for Christ's sake hath forgiven you" (Ephesians 4:32 KJV).

When Mephibosheth is called before King David, he probably thinks his day of reckoning has finally come. Due to the bad teaching he has received regarding the king, he no doubt thinks that justice has finally caught up with him. What he doesn't realize is that he is right: justice has caught up with him. Due to the covenant, justice demands that Mephibosheth be provided for, even though he doesn't deserve it. Mephibosheth is about to be a recipient of the New Covenant in an Old Covenant world.

Read the ninth chapter of 2 Samuel sometime, and bask in the beauty of the encounter between these two biblical characters. What you will notice is that David is not at all hostile toward the grandson of the man who had pledged to kill him. He even states that Mephibosheth can eat at his table as if he is one of his own sons (verse 11)!

"So Mephibosheth dwelt in Jerusalem, for he ate continually at the king's table. And he was lame in both his feet" (2 Samuel 9:13).

This story closes with a stark reminder that Mephibosheth's walk will neither hamper nor hinder the grace of David toward him. Believer, let's remind the next generation that God is not mad and that He has dealt with them through His covenant of kindness. Let's point them to the cross, where they can see a vivid display of God's justice toward their sin and His love toward their life. And finally, let's let our next generations know that the grace of God is not dependent on whether they live perfect lives. Their Father doesn't give them good things based on their daily walk, but He does so because of their faith in Christ. He does nothing for their sake; He does everything for Christ's sake!

Remove the Unholy Fear

Every parent has had to convince their child, at least once, that there were no monsters in the house or boogeyman under the bed. Children are easily scared by the dark, the shadows, or even a room that is too quiet. We do all we can to alleviate those fears, going so far as to open closet doors and peek under the bed for them. We all want our children to feel safe and secure, confident there is nothing that can harm them.

Our Heavenly Father is a better parent than all of us. He, too, desires His children to feel safe and secure in the finished work of Jesus and that we no longer distance ourselves from Him out of dread. Can you imagine the pain you would feel if you came home to hug your daughter and she shrank away out of fear you were going to hit her instead? How must the Father feel when His children shrink away and call it a "holy fear"?

Truthfully, this type of fear is far from holy, for it inadvertently acts as if the sacrifice of Jesus at Calvary did nothing to appease God. Rather than showing ourselves holy through this fear, we are showing that we are woefully misinformed at best and downright insulting at worst!

An unholy fear of God causes us to never be, "loosed and let go." It makes us constantly conscious of sin and places our attention and focus on hell instead of heaven. Jesus' victory over Satan was not only a victory over our enemy but also over our bondage. Look at what the author of Hebrews says immediately following the statement about Christ overcoming the devil:

"And release those who through fear of death were all their lifetime subject to bondage" (Hebrews 2:15).

This type of fear places us back in bondage, just like we were before we were born again.

"But the Bible says to work out our salvation with fear and trembling. Don't you think we should fear and tremble before a thrice holy God?"

I do believe that God is holy, and I do believe that an awareness of that holiness will cause us to fear and tremble. What I *don't* believe is the fearing and trembling we are being encouraged to do by the Apostle Paul have anything to do with a fear of judgment or death. Letting the tried and true method of letting the Bible interpret the Bible, we notice that not all fear and trembling is a bad thing.

"Then it shall be to Me a name of joy, a praise, and an honor before all nations of the earth, who shall hear all the good that I do to them; they shall *fear and tremble* for all the goodness and all the prosperity that I provide for it" (Jeremiah 33:9).

Note that the nations of the world will, "fear and tremble," not when they see the anger of God but when they notice all of the, "goodness and all the prosperity," God provides. Wow!

Also, watch again as the woman with the issue of blood approaches Jesus, touches the hem of His garment, and hears Him ask, "Who touched me?"

"But the woman, *fearing and trembling,* knowing what had happened to her, came and fell down before Him and told Him the whole truth" (Mark 5:33).

Her fearing and trembling was due to knowledge of the law. She knew that she had disobeyed the law of God by touching someone in her unclean state, and she was afraid that Jesus was going to call her on it. Had she had knowledge of grace, she might not have had such a response. Either way, Jesus responds to her fear not by applauding her for good Christian character but by calling her "Daughter."

While we are discussing it, let's look at Paul's statement about fear and trembling, including the verse that comes after it.

"Therefore, my beloved, as you have always obeyed, not as in my presence only, but now much more in my absence, *work out* your own salvation with fear and trembling; for it is God who *works in* you both to will and to do for His good pleasure" (Philippians 2:12, 13).

We work out of us what God is working in us. It's that simple. There is no working to be saved or to stay saved, rather a working to the outside what God has changed on the inside. Allow the awe that comes with seeing that God is good to remain in your life always, enabling you to bring to the surface all of the things that God is doing according to His will in your heart.

I have heard testimonies (and someone reading this may be the same way) of people who say they felt better being a sinner than they do as a Christian under the constant demand of do's and dont's. This mentality has led some Christians to believe that unbelievers are the free ones, able to do as they please, when they please. Satan has sold us a bill of goods if we believe this lie! Church, it is time that we proclaim the message of grace and freedom so loudly that it becomes obvious to whom the true liberty belongs.

The more you understand and accept the grace of God, the more you will rest in a true, "fear and trembling," of His goodness. After the author of Hebrews explained the difference between living at Mt. Sinai (Law) and living at Mt. Zion (Grace), he told what it will take to have this true, holy fear.

"Therefore, since we are receiving a kingdom which cannot be shaken, let us have grace, by which we may serve God acceptably with reverence and godly fear" (Hebrews 12:28).

Did you notice what the Apostle prayed we would have to enable us to serve God acceptably with godly fear? "Let us have grace!" The more grace you receive and walk in, the more you have true, godly fear. Any other fear is driven by the knowledge of the law and is an insult to the finished work of Christ.

"Pastor Paul, surely the story of Ananias and Sapphira teaches us that we should fear God! These two lied to the Holy Ghost, and God killed them, and this story is in the New Covenant. Doesn't this prove that God judges men for sin by killing them?"

Great question! Oh, how I wished someone had answered that question for me when I began to be introduced to the message of radical grace. I labored over Acts 5 day and night, longing for revelation concerning this story, sure that the answer was there but bothered at what I thought that it was implying.

I searched my commentaries in desperation, looking for some semblance of God's grace and favor. Unfortunately, most of the time, I was more confused and frightened than ever before. Most of the authors said the same thing, and it was twofold: Ananias and Sapphira were Christians, and God killed them to prove a point to the early church: if you sin badly enough, He will take out His judgment on you. Can you see why I was panicked?

With that in mind, let me make it perfectly clear: if God is killing Ananias and Sapphira here, (and Herod in Acts 12), for their sin, the message of, "It is finished," must be reevaluated. If He is killing them for sin, we are wrong to say that He judged all sin in the body of His Son on the cross. Also, if He is demonstrating His righteous judgment in these stories, we have true reason to fear that if we commit sin now then God might kill us, too.

I will start by declaring to you there is not a single instance in the New Testament of a believer being killed because of his sin and disobedience. Acts chapter 5, which relates the story of Ananias and Sapphira, never refers to them as "brother" or "sister" in the Lord, a very common trait of the book when dealing with believers. Also, the Scripture tells us that Peter points out that Satan had filled their hearts to lie to the Holy Ghost, a characteristic that *cannot* mark a true believer. Satan cannot fill your heart if Jesus is on the throne, for you have invited Christ in, and He won't share!

Now we know that wicked Herod isn't a believer in Acts 12, so that's not much of an issue. But, the question still remains as to whether God was judging them for their sin by killing them. Aside from the fact that they are not believers, didn't Christ die at Calvary for the sins of the world, even for the sins of Ananias, Sapphira, and Herod? If so, why are they apparently dying for those sins as well?

Death is not a part of judgment. I emphasize that sentence so you will realize how important it is to this story. Men die, not as a result of the judgment of God, but as the end result of sin. The Greek text says that we all have a "reservation" with death: "And it is appointed (reserved) unto men once to die, but after this the judgment" (Hebrews 9:27 KJV). The appointment with death comes first and then comes the judgment. These are two distinct events, not to be confused with one another.

Jesus set the date of the judgment of men who reject Him as the last day as well, separate from their death. "'He who rejects Me, and does not receive My words, has that which judges him - the word that I have spoken will judge him in the last day'" (John 12:48). Jesus can't set man's Day of Judgment as "the last day" and then pour out judgment on man now, can He?

If death is not a part of judgment, from where does it come? Think of sin as a seed inside of the heart of every man. Without the redeeming, transformative blood of Jesus, that seed will grow and produce horrific works of flesh and darkness. Just as a tree grows and produces fruit, sin will grow and produce a fruit of its own. However, when sin is completely finished inside of a vessel, it has a dangerous by-product that must come forth.

"Then when lust has conceived, it brings forth sin: and sin, when it is finished, brings forth death" (James 1:15 KJV).

The phrase, "it is finished," appears twice in the New Testament. Once on the cross, when Jesus cries out just before dying, and here in the book of James. The first usage, in John 19:30, is the Greek word *teleo* and it means, "to execute, to fulfill, or to end." In James, it is the word "apoteleo," which means "to end when you reach a goal." When Jesus said, "It is finished," He was declaring that the law was fulfilled, and the war against sin had come to an end. When James said, "it is finished," he was referring to sin reaching its goal in someone's life: death.

Several chapters ago, we dealt with living beneath one of two doctrines, either sin leading to death or obedience leading to righteousness. Go back to chapter 11 and freshen up on that topic if necessary, because I want you to remember that believers are living under the latter, not the former. Unbelievers are constantly beneath sin leading to death, which is why their sin ultimately leads to death.

I'm not insinuating that believers don't die a physical death, because as we have already read, all men die. However, if the end result of sin coming to its goal is the death of the host, believers should live the longest, right? Our old man has been crucified with Christ, and we are no longer servants to sin, thus, we can see long life because of the grace of God.

Our three characters in the book of Acts are all unbelievers, which means they were living beneath the law of sin and death. Their sin, though paid for by the blood of Jesus, was still leading them down a rapid course toward death, because they had not placed their faith in Christ. Ultimately, what did them in was not God striking them with judgment but their sin reached its sum, and death was followed naturally.

I know this answer doesn't completely satisfy our longing to know why, because we still see God's hand very heavily in these deaths. We need to remember an important point we have made elsewhere but have not placed much emphasis on. Let's read it again in Scripture and notice the highlighted portion.

"Inasmuch then as the children have partaken of flesh and blood, He Himself likewise shared in the same, that *through death He might destroy him who had the power of death,* that is, the devil" (Hebrews 2:14).

Jesus' death destroyed the devil's power, and notice what his greatest power was: "the power of death." If Satan had the power of death and Jesus' death took that away, we can be certain God is the only one who holds the power of death. No one lives or dies without God's knowledge. This doesn't mean God kills him, but, rather, God holds the power of life and death in His hands.

One more vital piece of information I want you to remember: men do not go to hell for their sins; they go to hell for the sin of rejecting Jesus. In fact, the Holy Spirit doesn't convict men of their individual acts of sin in order to lead them to Christ. Instead, He convicts them of the sin of not believing in Jesus (John 16:9). For someone to reject the conviction of the Holy Spirit over and over is for him to repeatedly tell Him no. This is a dangerous place to live!

Man can deny there is a God and deny that Jesus is God's Son, and neither of these things will bring on death. But to repeatedly deny the calling of the Holy Spirit in their heart toward salvation is what Jesus called blasphemy of the Holy Spirit (Mark 3:29). This is the only thing that is unforgiveable, for to reject His calling is to seek justification of your own merit and works.

This is the sin that John called, "the sin unto death" (1 John 5:16). It has to be, because we see Ananias, Sapphira, and Herod all die at the hands of God. Though God doesn't actually kill them (their sin led to a premature death), He holds the power of life and death in His hands, so man lives and dies at His mercy. These three had simply gone as far as man can go in rejecting the call of the Holy Spirit, and death is the only thing left.

None of us know by looking or talking to someone if he has had his absolute final rejection of the Holy Spirit's call. I like to say that as long as someone is still breathing, he has a chance to say yes to Jesus. However, many people are becoming calloused to the Holy Spirit's call, and only He knows how far gone their hearts are toward ever accepting Him. As is obvious from the text, God can certainly speed the process along, not as judgment, but as sin's end result.

If the examples of Ananias, Sapphira, and Herod had convinced the early church that God was in the business of killing people for their sins, surely they would have warned us of this in their epistles. Instead, they consistently pointed to Jesus as the propitiation for all sins, quick to bring glory to His finished work. They understood that sin brought forth death, and this is why they worked so hard to bring life into their readers.

One more thing of beauty I have to emphasize so that my Jesus is made lovely at the end of an extended passage on sin and death. Notice that when Jesus said, "It is finished," He brought life to mankind. But when sin has its own, "it is finished," it brings forth death. Jesus', "It is finished," rolled the stone away from the door of death; sin's, "it is finished," rolls a stone over the door of death. What a difference our Jesus makes!

Beloved, I trust you won't just take my word for it regarding the many things that we have covered in this book. I had to search the Scriptures and find confirmation in my heart for these words, and I am confident that I have found the heart of God. However, you must know it in your own heart as well, and you must be convinced, not by the persuasiveness of the speaker, but by the truth of the Word. If you do not see it in the Word, don't buy it; however, be equally quick to accept what His Word bears out.

I hope I have properly stressed how important it is that we get things right as they regard the attitude of our God. We have an entire generation just waiting for us to show up with some truth and hope. Grace is that message, and it is transformative beyond our wildest dreams. It is the message of the hour and, I believe, the message of the *final* hour. For such a time as this, we have been raised up to proclaim the glorious grace of our God. Prepare yourself, for now that you are armed with this knowledge, you may have a job to do as well!

Conclusion

We started this journey together in order to see change in our lives, not a superficial change, but a permanent one that springs from the inside out. Together, we have journeyed through the Word, found Jesus to be lovely, and have ended at the foot of His cross, resting in His grace and favor. The seeds of change have been planted, and I believe they are already beginning to sprout forth in your heart.

I find it necessary to put a capstone on this book as a way of sealing the sum of all that has been shared. To do so, I want to establish a few more truths in your heart as a way of equipping you for what happens when you finish the last page and go about your business.

Any and all change that has happened in you, and will continue to happen in you, comes as a result of the finished work of Christ on the cross. The prophet Zechariah saw a mountain of opposition to the rebuilding of the Jewish temple in Jerusalem, and he stated what I don't want you to forget:

> "'Not by might nor by power, but by My Spirit,' says the LORD of hosts" (Zechariah 4:6).

No human might or power can affect permanent change and remove mountains of doubt, insecurity, or other obstacles. Only the work of the Spirit within us can do what Zechariah prophesied to the head builder of the temple, a man named Zerubbabel.

> "Who are you, O great mountain? Before Zerubbabel you shall become a plain! And he shall bring forth the capstone with shouts of 'Grace, grace to it!'" (Zechariah 4:7).

The mountain of problems that used to define you is going to become a plain in front of your very eyes, and the way to bring this about is with shouts of "Grace!" The prophet believed in speaking what was needed in a particular situation. You have learned great truths about who you are in Christ and who Christ is in you. Begin to speak aloud these things in the presence of your obstacle, and allow grace to finish the work.

The early church believed in the wonderful power of this grace, and they often used the ability to speak His grace into their situation and into the lives of their followers. Look at the final words of some of the greatest apostles: Paul, Peter, and John.

"The Lord Jesus Christ be with your spirit. *Grace* be with you. Amen" (2 Timothy 4:22).

"But grow in the *grace* and knowledge of our Lord and Savior Jesus Christ. To Him be the glory both now and forever. Amen" (2 Peter 3:18).

"The *grace* of our Lord Jesus Christ be with you all. Amen" (Revelation 22:21).

I emphasized the key word in each apostle's closing statement. They all spoke grace into the lives of the listener, for they obviously understood the power of receiving the free gift of God's grace and favor in every possible situation.

"And since we have the same spirit of faith, according to what is written, 'I believed and therefore I spoke,' we also believe and therefore speak" (2 Corinthians 4:13).

They were quick to say what they believed. Be as quick to vocalize what you know to be true about Christ's finished work in your life.
Do you believe you are His righteousness? Say it! Do you believe He has finished the work? Say it! Satan can't read your mind, so let him hear your confession of your Father's goodness.

Notice that each writer also ends with the same word, "Amen." We are accustomed to using it at the end of our prayers, but I would dare say most Christians don't really understand why they do so. Remember that Christ has paid for everything, even the blessings attached to the keeping of the law that we can't keep. All of it is in Him. If that is the case, all promises are in Him as well. To appropriate those promises on a daily basis, let's know them and speak them.

"For the promises of God in Him are Yes, and in Him Amen, to the glory of God through us" (2 Corinthians 1:20).

When we proclaim, "Amen," we are agreeing with the promises of God, which are paid for through Jesus Christ. In fact, the word itself literally means, "so be it unto me." The apostles were not only speaking grace into our lives, they were sealing it with the power of the "amen," honoring Christ's finished work!

Leave the Lid on It

We all have things in our past that we aren't happy about, but we are certainly glad they are in our past and not still in our lives. Let's leave what is behind us and move on to the great things that God has in store for us.

"Brethren, I do not count myself to have apprehended; but one thing I do, forgetting those things which are behind and reaching forward to those things which are ahead, I press toward the goal for the prize of the upward call of God in Christ Jesus" (Philippians 3:13, 14).

The Philistines, mortal enemy to Israel, once stole the Ark of the Covenant from the Tabernacle. God cursed the thieves with a nasty case of hemorrhoids, which prompted them to send the Ark back to Israel on a cart, pulled by two cows. When the Ark arrived in the village of Bethshemesh, the priests took it off the cart and sacrificed the cows to the Lord. Next, something tragic occurred.

"And He struck the men of Bethshemesh, because they had looked into the ark of the LORD. He struck fifty thousand and seventy men of the people" (1 Samuel 6:19).

Years ago, when I first read this story, I thought, *Wow, that seems a little harsh doesn't it? God killed over fifty thousand people just because they looked inside of the Ark of the Covenant.* Then I realized the reason for God's anger.

The Ark of the Covenant was covered with the blood of a spotless lamb, offered every year as the payment for the sins of Israel on the Day of Atonement. This sacrifice pushed the wrath of God back another year. It is the sacrifice that we spoke of earlier, from Hebrews chapter 10.

The blood signified God's appeasement, covering the place of His anger and fury. To remove the lid was to look past the blood at brokenness and error. God had placed the blood as His barrier, and no man has the right to look past what Christ has paid for.

You need not fear God striking you down if you peer past the blood of Jesus, but please note the importance of honoring the blood above everything else. His blood is more powerful than your past, your present, and your future. Jesus' finished work is greater than your ability to sin, to fail, and to give up. What Christ has done is never to be looked on lightly nor deemed insufficient. God wanted no man to lift the lid and look beyond the blood. He wants all eyes to focus on the blood of His Son.

Leave the lid on your past, and see Jesus as your present possession. Due to what Christ has done, you no longer have reason to fear for tomorrow, because He is waiting there for you as well. Keep your eyes focused on who He is and what He has done. Don't panic if you see symptoms of your old self, rearing their ugly head. Assert who you are in Christ, and know that none of that changes just because you slip. Be that lamb that, if it falls into the mud, wants to be clean, rather than the pig that falls in the mud and feels at home.

I am so honored to have walked this road with you, sharing the things that God has revealed to me through studying His Word, hearing sermons of His love, and staring directly at the image of His lovely Son. Take what you have learned and, "love life and see good days" (1 Peter 3:10). Be prepared to roll the stone away from the life of someone else, while never lifting the lid off of his sin.

Go and grow, my dearly beloved. You have seen Jesus, and now let others see Him through you.

CPSIA information can be obtained
at www.ICGtesting.com
Printed in the USA
LVHW111940031218
598757LV00013B/10/P